*One Bullet for Me*

# ONE BULLET FOR ME

*Magdalene Krüger Klinksiek*
with Janet M. Hixon

The emblem of the city-state of Danzig

Christian Publications, Inc.
Camp Hill, Pennsylvania

Christian Publications
3825 Hartzdale Drive
Camp Hill, PA 17011

*Faithful, biblical publishing since 1883*

ISBN: 0-87509-678-6
LOC Catalog Card Number: 96-85144

© 1996 by Christian Publications

96  97  98  99  00    5  4  3  2  1

This book is lovingly dedicated

to **Gunter**
my faithful, God-given husband

to **Karl, Peter, Margaret** and **Susan**
and their spouses,
our dear children
who are so close to our hearts,
to whom our heavenly Father
graciously gave

**all our precious, so-lovable
grandchildren.**

## Table of Contents

Strathroy Middlesex
General Hospital

SMGH

The Building Together Campaign
"Your Hospital, Your Community"
visit our website – www.smghfoundation.on.ca

# Foreword

$\mathcal{T}$he book you hold in your hand is a reminder of God's faithfulness to one family during the Nazi era. Throughout that time when millions simply assumed that God had withdrawn from His people, there were those who discovered His guidance even in minute details. This story is a powerful witness to the promise, "I will never leave thee, nor forsake thee" (Hebrews 13:5).

Those of us who have studied World War II often focus on Hitler's rise to power, his hypnotic effect on much of Europe and the sequence of events as the war unfolded. We forget that God was working in individual lives even as He does today, giving comfort and direction. While we look at history as various discernible stages among the masses, God keeps His focus on those whose names are written in the book of life.

Magdalene Klinksiek had the good fortune of being born into a Christian family that lived to prove God's loving care even in the midst of a country that had been swallowed up by the euphoria of Hitler. From the early beginnings of her humble home in Danzig, she saw the reality of the Christian faith demonstrated in the lives of her parents and grandparents. This gave her confidence to believe that God could be trusted—even when she was surrounded by the fearful events of a world at war.

Magdalene's marriage to Gunter in 1950 was the beginning of a new stage in her life. Together they would serve the Lord, not realizing that someday their ministry would touch the lives of thousands of believers in churches across North America. In retrospect, God has done more for them than they might have imagined.

Music played a special part in Magdalene's life from earliest childhood. Whether it was a hymn she learned or a melody that was born in her own heart, Magdalene has always had a song on her lips. So it was only natural that when God worked mightily in their hearts during a period of revival in the 1970s, they began to travel to various churches sharing their testimony and singing the praises of the Lord.

We have all been blessed by their ministry. Whether in German or in English, the lyrics to their songs have always been focused on Christ. Their motto might well be:

Jesus is the most beautiful name,
Above all names on earth

Nothing can compare with Him,
And all the glory His.

As you read this book, you will agree that this couple does indeed give God all the glory. Magdalene and Gunter will go on serving their Lord until they see Him face to face. Through this book, we too can be a part of their journey.

Dr. Erwin W. Lutzer
February 1996

# Acknowledgments

---

There are too many friends and dear people I was allowed to meet personally over the last twenty years to name here, people who encouraged me to write down all I had shared in various meetings. There are so many who prayed that this book would soon come to completion. To all of you, my deepest thanks and a big hug.

Were it not for the patient work and marvelous leading of my dear Lord, my heavenly Father and His Holy Spirit, teaching and guiding this frail vessel, I would have nothing worthwhile to share. He wrote into my life the pages that are before you. Freed like a bird from a dark cage, I followed His Word from Deuteronomy 8:2: "And thou shalt remember all the way which the LORD thy God led thee." To Him goes my deepest gratitude, praise and adoration: *All glory be His.* I also thank Him and each one who was willing to have a part in the long process of bringing this book project together.

There is my dear husband—thank you, Gunter, for always considering my need for quiet as

I wrote. Thank you for the refreshments, for the coaxing to get out for a walk in the woods and for your God-given patience during these years with me. Thank you, *schatz!*

Thank you, Edith and Thomas, for the quiet room with the special window looking onto the hills of Montana where I penned more of the book in a time of rest during crusades.

The same thank you to so many of our hosts on crusades for a place I could write on our days off.

Thank you to Charlotte Ruby, who was the first one to type for me. Only the long distance to the state of Washington hindered your commitment.

But my greatest gratitude goes to Janice MacKenzie, my dear friend and spiritual daughter, who with unending dedication and sacrificial patience listened for countless hours, week after week, to the many tapes of my German-accented voice. You called it a privilege to give so much precious time for this project, were not willing to be reimbursed in any way, supplied freely everything that was needed—and typed for the first time into an unfamiliar computer! Without you, the book could never have reached the publisher. I can only say the Lord will richly reward what you have done unto Him and me. Thank you to the entire MacKenzie family, who freed Mum whenever I needed her for typing or other requests for the book.

My great appreciation also goes to Ralph and Lou Sutera and Dr. Erwin Lutzer for their encouragement and recommendation to go on with the book, and to Dr. Neill Foster, who so wisely changed the book's title just before it went to the printer.

A special thank you to my dear editor, Janet Hixon from Christian Publications, who with much skill and loving understanding supported me during the last stages to bring this book to completion.

In all this, *thank you, Lord,* for all your guidance. Because of him who said, "I will never leave thee, nor forsake thee" (Hebrews 13:5),

*Magdalene Kindsich*

*One Bullet for Me*

# CHAPTER 1

# *The War Begins*

*It is better to trust in the LORD than to put
confidence in man. (Psalm 118:8)*

*W*hy are the church bells ringing? was my
first thought when I was awakened
abruptly that morning.

I loved to hear the church bells ringing, their
beautiful, deep melodic sounds filling the air of
our suburb nestled at the foot of the wooded
hills near Danzig, the last free city-state in
Europe. Located at the mouth of the Vistula
River by the Baltic Sea, Danzig was an old and
wealthy city. Close by was "the Corridor" or
"the Passage," a long, neutral stretch of land
leading to Poland and Germany.

We Danzigers had our own currency, the
*Gulden*; we had our own postage stamps; we
had our own flag. We had at least 400,000 citi-

zens in the immediate city and suburbs and a few thousand in the bordering rural areas of the lowland; we also had our own passports as citizens of the Free State of Danzig.

I had lived there in the Danzig suburb of Langfuhr at Luisental #8 all twelve years of my life. My father worked in the customs office and supported our family—which consisted of my parents, my three sisters, my two brothers and me.

But this morning the beautiful bells rang so early. . . . And thundering and grumbling in the distance was a sound that made our house shiver. What was going on?

We jumped out of bed. My seventeen-year-old brother Karl ran out of the house and took off on his bicycle. About half an hour later, when the church bells stopped ringing, we could hear more clearly than before the sound of continuous explosions. We got dressed, waiting for whatever would follow.

My grandparents and uncle, who lived in two front rooms of our home, came over to pray with us for God's protection on our family—wherever they were at the time. My oldest brother Heinz was a teacher and lived away from home, and my sisters Ruth and Anneliese were also away at school. Not long after that prayer my papa arrived, but my brother was still missing.

The sound of a big explosion made our

house shake for a moment. "It sounds like war," said my father, who had been a soldier in the First World War.

My uncle turned the radio on. The announcer said that the German battleship *Schleswig-Holstein* had attacked the Westerplatte, the peninsula near the harbor of Danzig, where the Poles had enlarged their arsenal in preparation for war. And we heard our free city-state of Danzig was no longer separated from the Fatherland and was free to come into the Reich.

I remembered in the previous weeks before this we learned a new song in school:

> Germany, Motherland, when are you taking us back?
> Germany, Fatherland, stand against our fate!
> We're waiting here at Vistula's shore,
> Enduring here in dunes and sand.
> One day a red rising sun will glow o'er night and death,
> One day a red rising sun will start the day for us.

Repeatedly we had heard the slogans of propaganda: "We want to go home into the Reich." *Why would we want to do that?* we wondered. We had everything we needed and loved, much more than those who came to visit us from Germany. Every year tourists came

through the Corridor to see the countless art
treasures of our city, to vacation at the beach
resorts and to enjoy the wooded hills and the
famous forest opera grounds near the Baltic Sea
town of Zoppot.

"Papa, are we now free? Are we Germans
now?" I asked. I was a little unsure what it
meant to be German.

"Magda, what language do you speak?" he
asked.

"German."

"Haven't you been free?"

"Yes," I answered, but I didn't understand.

Late that afternoon my brother came back
and reported what he had seen. There was a
huge fire from all the explosions and shooting.

He had tried to get closer to the beach and
the Westerplatte near the harbor but was repeatedly stopped by the police. The streets
were almost empty. A mixture of shock and
fear had gripped our ancient, peaceful city.

Though Papa was angry that Karl had left
without asking permission and had caused
Mama much concern, his stern face showed
understanding—he had been a soldier once.

It was September 1, 1939—the first day of
World War II was coming to an end. That evening our family devotional time had a special
effect on me. While all of us knelt down in
prayer as usual, I felt the sure, protecting love
of God over our family.

The next day I was allowed to go outside.
As fast as my feet would carry me I ran out
the winding path to my beloved lookout, the
*Karls Hoehe.* There was seldom a day that I did
not go there beneath the cathedral-like ceiling
of the beech trees and sigh at the beauty of
the view. But today I was dismayed at the
sight that I had tried to imagine after hearing
my brother's report: black clouds of smoke
hung over the right side of our beach resort,
Broesen. I could not identify anything else. A
yellowish-gray veil was hanging over the
Westerplatte.

I looked to the right. There stood the majestic
Lutheran church with its high, slim tower, filling the large corner lot of Johannesberg, the
street parallel to ours, which also led up to the
woods. My eyes glanced further past the main
street. There was our well-known Women's
Clinic, where I was born, with the famous stork
on top of the roof.

As far as I could see, everything seemed to be
all right. My eyes wandered farther over to the
beach resort of Broesen. I had often come here
to watch which of its many faces the Baltic Sea
would show that day—would white foam on
high waves roll onto the beach? Would the sea
bring forth a harvest more generous than usual
of glistening amber stones, jewels only to be
found on the beaches of the Baltic Sea near
Danzig? Or would it lie quiet and calm, shim-

mering like a diamond, lined by the sparkling, golden-white sand?

My thoughts were interrupted by a roar that came close within seconds. Bewildered, I looked up. A squadron of planes raced over the towering beech trees above me. One by one they flew down toward the coastline, releasing groups of what looked to me like shining silver eggs. A huge explosion followed. Flames and smoke mingled, blocking the view of the coastline.

I was stunned and shocked. Again and again they returned; there was no pause. For a moment I thought the coast would break apart and the mighty waters would rush over the land.

More people had come up to the forest by that time, and they too stood watching that gigantic operation of destruction. Suddenly I remembered my parents; they would be worried that I was still outside. I ran home and shared what I had seen. Later on we heard over the radio that the bunkers on the Westerplatte were burning out. The German bomber planes, the famous *Stukas,* had finished their devastating work. The great Polish port of Gdingen had also been attacked.

Soon after, glued to the radio, we heard the heart-chilling voice of Adolf Hitler himself declaring that Danzig was no longer separated from its fatherland, but had been taken "home," back into Great Germany.

"Papa," I asked, "What does this mean?"

"We will no longer be a free city-state, having independence and all that goes with it. We will have to wait and see," he replied with uncertainty.

The Second World War had started here, in our beloved city-state of Danzig.

Only a day or two later the radio aired another speech by Adolf Hitler. I listened to the loud voice of the man they called *Der Fuehrer*. It sounded very scary to me. He replaced the name "God the Almighty" with *die Vorsehung* (our fate), which was leading him and us into a new era of time.

My brother was constantly on the go, watching what was going on around town. One day he came home with some news that shocked us all.

The Jewish synagogue in our peaceful suburb had had its windows and doors smashed in, and our big department store, Sternfeld, was closed up because the owners were Jews. I will never forget my mother's sad face. "Oh, these poor Jews. May God have mercy on them and on us. When the enemy gets at God's chosen people, it will not take long to get at the Christians."

I ran over to visit my girlfriend, Ursula Rosenthal. We had not seen each other for several days. I rang the doorbell of the apartment and heard some loud voices inside. I wished I had not come. As I turned to leave, Ursula opened the door and pulled me inside. I heard the voice of Dr. Rosenthal pleading with his wife to open her bedroom door, which she had locked.

"Oh, they argue often," Ursula explained. I felt very uncomfortable and wanted to leave. Ursula's mother was an Arian who had been married before. Her son from that marriage had joined the SS (Hilter's special police). He asked his mother to leave her Jewish husband. Since then Ursula's parents were always fighting.

It was so confusing. We sat there for a little while on her bed, my arm around her, trying to take her mind off the situation. "Remember the little bantam chickens we had so much fun with?" I asked. My Aunt Mariechen had given me a little rooster and hen for my birthday. Mama was not really too pleased about this because they refused to stay in the back yard. Instead they would fly over or squeeze under the fence that separated the back yard from the front one—where Mama had all her beautiful half-moon flower beds.

"Remember how we tried to catch them?" I giggled. Ursula and I, in our eagerness, had almost fallen into the flowers before we managed to capture them. Eve, the little hen, was breathing very hard, and we sneaked her into the living room while Mama was working outside. While Ursula held the rooster, Eve cuddled up in the corner of the red velvet armchair. There, before our wide eyes, she laid her very first egg.

"Yes," Ursula smiled, "and we tried to keep her from announcing her success so your mother wouldn't hear that we were in the living room!" We both tried to suppress our giggles.

Glad to help my friend remember happier times, I encouraged her, "You'll see. Something will work out, I'm sure."

School started again and we were told *Der Fuehrer* would come to Danzig to see the city, and all students were to go to welcome him. We had to wear white blouses with black triangled scarves tied in the front with a leather knot.

All people were asked to hang a new red flag out of their windows—a flag that had a strange symbol in the middle, a round white circle with a cross with hooks, which they called the *Haken kreuz*—swastika. We marched the three-kilometer-long famous Linden Allee, which stretched from our suburb of Langfuhr to Danzig. The historical buildings, hundreds of years old, were decorated with flags; green garlands and wreaths adorned with the strange sign of the swastika. Big signs hung over the streets: "We greet our *Fuehrer* who freed us." We marched down the Langasse, which led past the beautiful historic city hall with the high, slim tower and the golden windguard on its tips. All these houses once belonged to the wealthy patricians, the merchant princes who had governed the area. These same patricians had brought both historic values and riches into Danzig.

After arriving close to the Lang Market at city hall, some of us tried to secure a spot on the stairs to have a good look down the Langasse, where hundreds spread out to line the streets. But after a while we had to move again, as thousands of students had to find a place to stand and wait.

Finally, with all kinds of troops marching in and taking our places, I ended up in one of the ancient historical buildings, the Stocktower, a former prison about 400 years old. An emergency Red Cross station was set up there and one of the attendants told us to go up to the higher floors. We walked up the dark, spooky stairs, looking into the naked prison cells with the heavy chains bolted into the walls, into the old torture chamber with the stocks and heavy iron balls and chains that were once used to keep the prisoners within these damp, cold walls. Climbing up another flight of cold rocky stairs, we saw light shining through some corridors that finally led us to the open, barred windows hewn into the stony wall.

Pulling ourselves up by the iron bars, we climbed onto the windowsills, and soon we heard the sound of march music accompanying the SS troops coming around the Coal Market and passing the city theater toward the Stock-tower where we were standing.

There, in a black, shiny convertible, sur-rounded by walking security officers, stood the man called Adolf Hitler. An excited shout of, "Heil Hitler!" echoed and carried to where we were standing. He looked at the hundreds of people lining the streets, and he also looked up to the old historic buildings—right at us, it seemed.

His right arm was always lifted up, while his stern face had moved to take in the celebration. A cold, strange feeling of fear overwhelmed me.

The procession headed toward the Lang Market, accompanied by the marching troops, music and voices shouting, "Heil, Heil, Heil!" The noise died down as the crowds waited to hear him give his scheduled speech. We climbed down from our positions and were told to get up to the Bischofs Berg, one of the high hills surrounding the ancient city with its city walls, high watchtowers and winding lanes. Other students had gathered there, and we were instructed to line both sides of the long driveway, building a human wall of wel-coming students. Now very close to the coming procession, we heard sounds of fanfare and drums. The convertible turned into the driveway. My heart pounded. Again a strange mixture of fear and tension came over me as he drove about two feet away from me through the rows of shouting, excited students throwing flowers into his car. He was smiling as he touched some of their outstretched hands. His piercing, hypnotic eyes searched through the crowd.

The war with Poland, officially called "The War of 18 Days," was finished, but expanded into other countries. Our school days were regular again and our daily life at home did not change much.

My girlfriend Ursula had not come back to school. When I went to her house to find out why, her father explained that she was not allowed to attend because she was half Jewish. At first I thought that they wanted to have nothing to do with the new government and that's why her father, a leading skin specialist, was sending her to a private school. Her mother had left them, and I was told they would be moving to Danzig where Dr. Rosenthal had his office. Seeing my disappointment at losing my special friend, Ursula comforted me by promising I could visit her on the weekends and stay overnight.

At school we felt the first changes incurred by the war. We had to learn to write German in a new way—the Latin way—because, we were told, one day the German language would be spoken all over the world. In biology we were introduced to Darwin's teaching. *How silly,* I thought, *to think we would come from a monkey!* Lifting my hand, I explained to the teacher that in the Bible, the creation report says God made us in His image.

The teacher, ignoring my remarks, said, "You will understand when you see that all living creatures developed gradually." Young as I was, I became very cautious about what to believe, and I knew where to take a stand when I had discussions with my classmates in the school yard.

Later more changes came to our school. A new religion was introduced—*Gottgläubig,* which means "God-believing." It replaced the Protestant and Catholic religious teachings.

Our new reading book was as thick as the Bible, entitled *Ewiges Deutschland*—"Eternal Germany." It had a picture of the *Fuehrer* on the first page. This book contained ballads, poems and stories of famous German writers and poets. There were also several slogans. One of the slogans was, "To fight a war against yourself is the hardest war. To have victory over self is the greatest victory."

There was a strong emphasis on high

achievement and progress in our country because of what the *Fuehrer* did for us. Every German family would soon have a Volks-wagen. Motherhood was highly honored. My mama, mother of six, received a Mother's Cross, and for the first time she was sent on a vacation. She also got a young student to help in the house.

We students had to stand in a circle around the new flag with a swastika (our own Danzig flag had disappeared). We learned new songs about our Fatherland, Germany, with beautiful melodies and harmonies. Every morning, with our right arms stretched out, we had to sing the *Horst Wessel Lied: Die Fahne Hoch* ("The Flag Up High," our new anthem).

I kept my arm down whenever I could. When I couldn't, I promised, *I lift my hand up for only You, God.*

# CHAPTER 2

# *Faith Becomes Conviction*

*Be thou faithful unto death, and I will give thee a crown of life. (Revelation 2:10)*

God had given me a special gift of music, and I could play any song by ear. One day when I was nine, my oldest brother Heinz (who was also very musically inclined) was playing my grandmother's piano and I was watching him. Seeing my interest, he showed me the three main harmonies—the first, fourth and fifth chords—in the key of E flat, which he always used in his songs. So I picked up three popular songs he brought home from teacher's college.

Shortly after that my mama sent me with some flowers to a new neighbor, an elderly lady,

Fraulein Fischbeck. The housekeeper opened the door and led me into the living room where a very tall, slim, darkly dressed lady was seated at the piano, playing the most beautiful music I had ever heard. I was spellbound.

She invited me to come in. Seeing my longing look toward the piano, she asked, "Do you play?"

"Yes," I said.

"What is your name?" she asked.

"Magdalene, but most of the time I am called Magda."

"Play something for me," she replied, getting up from the stool.

I played, "When You Are in Hawaii," "Under the Pinien of Argentina" and "I Danced with You into Heaven."

"Where did you learn these songs?" she demanded disapprovingly.

"From my oldest brother," I replied.

"Do you read any music?"

"No," I said.

"Well," she remarked thoughtfully, "you come and I will show you how to play the right way. Do not tell this to anyone."

When I came the next Saturday she had a book with notes on the piano, but before she started to teach me she held my hands and prayed, "Lord, let Magdalene's music be to Your glory only." But I did not understand what that meant.

My mother understood the special relationship between this lady and me and didn't mind that I went there almost every day after school. Realizing that God had given me a special musical gift, Fraulein Fischbeck gave in to my begging to play harder pieces.

And so we worked on "The Heavens Declare the Glory of God." When Christmas Eve finally arrived, our family gathered together to sing Christmas carols, and then Papa read the Christmas story from Luke, chapter 2. He closed with a thankful prayer for Jesus who came to the earth as a gift from God to a lost world. We were then asked for our contribution of poems or readings.

At last Mama asked, "Magda, do you have something for this Christmas Eve?" Hardly able to contain myself and blushing with excitement, I stepped forward to the pedal organ and for the first time in front of my family I played, "The Heavens Declare the Glory of God" by Joseph Haydn.

After the last chord had died down I stepped away from the bench. Tears ran down my father's face—I never had seen this before. He hugged me and pressed me close to his heart.

My father seemed to realize that music had a deep effect on me. One day, passing through the marketplace, I heard beautiful music being played by a military band. Forgetting everything, I listened—and came home a half an hour late. Everyone had finished eating dinner, and all eyes were on me as I entered the room, stammering an apology that I had listened to a gorgeous military band. With unusual softness in his voice Papa said only: "You will find food in the kitchen."

When I was almost fifteen years old, my parents took a family of five into our home. Their father, a fisherman, had died. I shared my bedroom with Liesel, the seventeen-year-old daughter. It was the first of May, around 9 p.m. We were about to go to bed when through the open window I heard again that beautiful military music.

"Liesel," I said. "The soldiers must march to the May Field for a night celebration. They are just three to four minutes up the road from us. Let's get dressed again and see."

Though we ran as fast as we could, we saw only the end of the band of trumpets, flutes and percussions, with the singing soldiers carrying lit torches. Rushing home to sneak upstairs again, we were surprised in the hall by Papa.

"Magda, come into the living room."

We sat down on the sofa.

"Where were you?" he demanded.

"To hear the military music band marching to the May Field."

His angry eyes softened.

"Do you realize that Mama and I were very upset and disturbed not finding both of you in your bedroom? There are great dangers out there for young girls like you. We have to know whenever you leave the house, no matter what."

"I am sorry," I said. "Please forgive me. I realize what we did was not right."

Getting onto his knees, Papa said, "Let us pray," and he asked the Lord to keep me in His ways and to give me an obedient, pure heart.

With tears in my eyes I hugged my dear father, never forgetting his loving concern for his youngest teenager.

---

During the summer months Fraulein Fischbeck took me to the huge St. Marien Church in Danzig to introduce me to the famous vesper organ concerts. The organ itself was famous, featuring 420 stops. But the cathedral was one of the largest in the world. In one corner of it you could hear a sevenfold echo, and the numerous sculptures, paintings and many altars designed by great artists left a deep impression on my heart. Fraulein Fischbeck's housekeeper always brought an extra blanket for me. Warmly wrapped up, my feet dangling from the hard, high benches, I marveled at the beautiful built-in chapels along the sides of the huge inner auditorium. They were all fenced in with only two or four benches inside. These belonged once to the rich merchants and patricians of Danzig, who preferred not to sit with the common people.

Within these high walls with the strong pillars and dome-like ceilings dotted with golden stars, the powerful music filled every corner— and also my heart. I often shivered under the God-inspired choral fugues and preludes of the great composer J.S. Bach. I knew deep inside that this man must have had a great love for God or he could never have written this heart-uplifting music, and a shy desire of hope grew in me to play the pipe organ in our own church one day for God's glory also.

It was about a year later when Mama and Fraulein Fischbeck took me to one of the other cathedrals to hear *Saint Matthew's Passion* by J.S. Bach. My heart was overwhelmed with a mixture of deep sorrow, adoration and thanksgiving that was expressed in these God-given melodies and harmonies that touched our souls. I felt that the whole city should have been there to hear such beautiful, inexpressible, moving music. On the way home, I was still deeply impressed by what I had heard and was not able to say anything. Mama said, "Magda, maybe one day when the war is over, you will have the chance to hear the beautiful music by Handel, the *Messiah*. It is not allowed since the new government. What glorifying music to our Lord that is."

And I wondered, *Why can't we hear it now?*

———⟪⟫———

I have had Jesus living in my heart since I was a young child, but I had a very special experience when I turned five.

On my birthday I had become very ill. After days of high fever, my legs became so weak that I could not walk. My mama totally wrapped me in wet sheets to sweat it out. My oldest sister, Ruth, read stories to me to pass the time, which seemed to me like many long hours. The fever gradually came down, but I was left with a lameness in my legs, which Mother, reading up in her homeopathic doctor books, diagnosed as polio. I was able to sit up in bed but unable to walk.

Then one day my mother brought a man and woman to my room. She said, "Magda, these people came to pray for you." They asked me if I believed that *der Liebe Heiland*, the dear Savior Jesus, could heal me so I could walk again. "Yes, I believe that," I said. Were not the first words which I learned in my prayer when I was a little child: "I am small, my heart keep pure, may no one live in it but Jesus alone"?

Jesus was already living in my heart, and having heard many Bible stories, I surely believed that He also could heal me. They helped me to sit up at the side of my bed and asked, "Will you try to walk?" At first a bit wobbly, I walked step by step across the room, feeling surer with every step. Oh, how they all thanked God for His blessings on me! Only some small weakness in my joints reminded me to wear leather support strips around my wrists when practicing piano until I would develop stronger muscles over the years.

My faith had grown stronger, too. Yet during this wartime, there seemed to be something wrong with me. I noticed that I did not have the joy I used to have. Sin had crept into my heart, and my conscience was no longer pure and clean. I was not quite sure that God still loved me. A fear and restlessness stirred my heart, though my bedtime prayers for some time had been: "Cover me with Thy wings, O Jesus. You're my joy. Keep Your little one when Satan wants to hurt me. Your angels keep around me; keep me from all harm."

But I knew I had given in to sin; there had been those little white lies, impure thoughts, anger and disobedience. I really never asked Jesus to forgive me for those things.

It was during the New Year's Eve midnight service in our Baptist church in Danzig that I desired to follow Him all my life. The Holy Spirit had repeatedly convicted me of sin in my heart. I had tried to erase it from my memory—but to no avail.

Refugees had begun to arrive in our city in the past year, and I began to fear. What would happen to me if we ever had to leave our beautiful city?

That night the pastor spoke about the uncertainty of the upcoming year of 1941, with the war getting broader and more fierce. Then we all went to prayer on our knees as the clock moved past midnight into the new year. There in quietness in my heart, I asked the Lord's forgiveness for all my sins, to wash them away and become my Savior. A peace and joy filled my heart as I thanked Him for forgiving me. From then on He would always live in me.

On the way home from church I could not contain myself. My heart was so light, so joyful that I felt like jumping ahead of my papa. I told him that I had asked the Lord Jesus to be my Savior and that I wanted to confess openly by baptism that I wanted to follow the Lord all my life. He was very, very happy. When I got home, I told Mama, who was not able to go because of her poor health. She said only, "May the Lord bless you, my child, and let you be a blessing."

Later, on the day of my baptism, the verse of Revelation 2:10 was given to me and confirmed my heart's desire: "Be thou faithful unto death, and I will give thee a crown of life." As I went down into the water, Romans 6:3-4 became real to me:

> Know ye not, that so many of us as were baptized into Jesus Christ were baptized into his death? Therefore we are buried with him by baptism into death: that like as Christ was raised up from the dead by the glory of the Father, even so we also should walk in newness of life.

That old Magdalene with all her sin had been left there in the watery grave. And my brothers and sisters in church now knew that I was living my new life with Him who had washed my sins away by His precious blood and was now living in me by His Holy Spirit. In the months to come, this assurance made me strong in my decisions and helped me stand against the influences of the political spirit that took hold of many of my classmates.

Under this new government, every young girl fourteen years and older was supposed to join the club of young German girls. Again the Lord provided a way out for me.

My dear Fraulein Fischbeck could no longer supervise my piano lessons; she was totally bedridden with arthritis. Through a letter of recommendation, I auditioned and was accepted by a concert pianist, Fraulein Krey, who taught at the music school in Danzig, called Gau Music School.

My parents made sure that there was no political influence at the music school. The only thing that was mentioned by my new piano teacher was that she was not allowed to teach anything by Mendelssohn-Bertholdy, who was a Jew. But she whispered, so as not to be heard, "What you play at home is up to yourself." She invited me to join her every week she was in town to attend piano or chamber concerts, and I gained much knowledge under her comments and instructions. Going to the Gau Music School saved me from going to the club of German girls. After receiving a written order to enlist in the local group of our area, I had to go to registration, not knowing what was waiting for me. I soon found out. We had to know where our *Fuehrer* came from, what he did for us and how he was faithfully surrounded by those who gave their lives for him in Munich, when Horst Wessel stepped in front of a bullet to die for his *Fuehrer*.

After doing some crafts and learning some new songs, we were dismissed. I knew that this group was not for me and stayed away the next time. I received repeated notices to attend. Finally my parents wrote a letter that I was much involved in the Gau Music School and its connected activities. They seemed to be satisfied with that, so I was free from attending. God was there with His hand again over me, preventing me from being influenced by such instruction.

The churches of born-again believers, like Baptists, Pentecostals, Brethren and others, were now under Great Germany, combined under a new name for better identification— Evangelical Freechurch Fellowship. They were separated from the state churches of Catholics and Protestants. Yet even within our Baptist church of about 400 members, some men had joined the new party, knowing it was now the only way to advance in their professions.

But one Sunday morning we were surprised with two Nazi flags on each side of the baptismal font. No one really knew who put them there or why, except that the next Sunday they were gone again. Then a church meeting was announced and those "brothers" who had brought in the swastika flags came forward, asking every member if they had removed them.

Getting to my grandfather they asked, "Opa Liedtke, did you take those flags away?"

"Yes, I did it," he said.

Doubting that he understood what they had asked him, they asked him again. "No, we want to know if you have taken the flags away."

"Yes," he said, "I did it, and if you put them there again, I will remove them again. They do not belong in God's house."

The result was a court order for him. My uncle's friend, a lawyer, wanted to defend his case, but Opa wanted to stand up for his Lord and King. The church was in prayer as my grandfather sat in the waiting room, waiting to get called in. He fell asleep and was awakened by my uncle. "Do I have to come in now?" he asked.

"No," was the reply. "You can go home. Your case is dismissed."

The Lord used the lawyer to defend my grandpa. He told the court that the old man did not understand the situation because of his old age. How my grandma hugged him when she had him back!

---

It was unofficially known that true Christians were on a blacklist. There seemed to be some secrecy going around in our house. Mama was seldom out of the house except for working in our flower garden, but I found her gone a few times when I came home from school. She kept this kind of secret. When I asked about some things I had seen—new linens with embroidery and strange initials and some beautiful bowls of silver—she let me in on the secret. She explained to me that a number of Jewish families were selling their valuables to get cash. Feeling very unsure of their safety, they wanted to leave the country to go to Palestine or England.

Our neighbors across the street tried to do the same. Mr. Wolf, a Jew, and his wife, an

Aryan lady, sold us a beautiful painting of Jesus praying on the Mount of Olives. It was
hung in our living room. I was later told that
Mr. Wolf's bank account was confiscated, and
he had no access to his money. Shortly after
that we heard that he hanged himself in the
attic.

After my piano lessons in the Gau Music
School in Danzig I often went to visit Ursula.
They lived a block down from the school in one
of the old patrician houses where her father
had his dermatology clinic. Going to visit her
one day after my lesson, I found her not at
home. When I inquired, Dr. Rosenthal said
only, "Ursula is not here. Come again next
week." He looked very grave and gave no further explanation. Where could she be? She was
the apple of her father's eye and had never
been away from him.

I thought this disappearance strange, but I
could hardly wait until my next piano lesson
was over. I rushed upstairs to the apartment.
Dr. Rosenthal opened the door. He looked very
old. I wondered why their maid was nowhere
to be seen. He asked me to come to his office
and sit across from his desk.

"Magda," he said, "do you see these two
books? One is a Bible and this is Hitler's *Mein
Kampf*. I have read both and I know what is going to happen to all Jews. For Ursula's sake I
could not tell you anything about her where-

abouts last week, but now she is safe with her aunt in England. You and your family have been good friends to her, and I want to thank you for that."

My heart was heavy as I sat in the last seat of the streetcar going home, trying to hide my tears.

A few days later the front page of our newspaper announced shocking news. Dr. Rosenthal, well-known skin specialist, had drowned in the Radaune River. His legs were found tied together.

*Oh, God,* I cried out in prayer, *what is going on?* He had been at our home just a little while before that, treating my Grandpa's eczema. He never took any fee; he was a man always there for others. My thoughts wandered to Ursula in England. Would she ever find out what had happened to her father?

All this was so confusing to me. What would we ever do without the comfort of God's Word and the family of God? I was so glad that our community churches had a prayer week involving special services during the first week of January. These gatherings strengthened our spiritual lives and fellowship with one another.

It was not long after that that another case disturbed our little street. With only nine houses on our street, we knew each other very well. One of our neighbors, Pastor Walter from the Lutheran church down at the street corner, was taken away by the Gestapo. Mama always was there for those who went through trials, and she took me with her to visit Mrs. Walter. With tears streaming down her face, Mrs. Walter told us what had happened.

Her husband had preached at the Sunday morning service on Acts 4:18-19, where Peter and John replied to the command not to speak of the name of Jesus, "Is it right to listen to you rather than God?"

After the congregation had left, two men in civilian clothes got up from the last bench, identifying themselves as Gestapo, and arrested him for influencing the congregation against the law and the government. Mama prayed with Mrs. Walter, laying the situation in God's omnipotent, merciful hands. Later she was notified that Pastor Walter was in the concentration camp in Dachau.

Because of losing his leg in the First World War, he had received a medal for bravery, so his punishment was reduced to office work in the concentration camp. Even men of the state church, as he was, were under the watchful eyes of the Nazi regime. Despite the impressive radio announcements of victories and the promising, powerful speeches of Adolf Hitler, we felt the strange, depressing atmosphere all around us.

# CHAPTER 3

# *Changes*

*To every thing there is a season, and a time to every purpose under the heaven. (Ecclesiastes 3:1)*

Life during the war was full of changes. Since we belonged to Great Germany, we also had to expect air raids, so blackout restrictions were enforced. Every building and home had to have blackout blinds so no light could be seen anywhere. Street lights were dimmed by black caps; car headlights were totally covered except for a one-inch crack, making driving very slow. The curbs of sidewalks were painted with phosphorous paint.

So people would not bump into each other, we wore lighting buttons. Some lucky ones had brooches attached to a little pocket battery. I had a little clown face that I could light up whenever I heard somebody approaching. It was fun but also sometimes kind of spooky. Suddenly in front of you a little figure could light up, and without recognizing the face or voice, you could be asked for directions.

Several times during the war the sirens sounded an alarm during the night, sending us for shelter into the basement, which was supplied with survival kits. Yet we experienced only one bomb attack, on one of our hospitals and surrounding houses. No other damage was done until the last week of the war in the spring of 1945.

My oldest brother Heinz, who had become a teacher, was drafted as an air defenseman on the ground, then transferred to Romania, and had been missing for some time. Later it was reported he had been taken to Russia as a prisoner. Karl, my younger brother, went through emergency examinations and through a quick training to become a teacher, but before long, he too was drafted and became a pilot on a fighter plane.

Watching my mother and father, I saw their strong yet humble faith in God as they left their two sons in His hands, never complaining about what He allowed for them. The last one at home now, I often heard Mama praying behind a closed door for all of us. And often I heard my own name being brought before God's throne of grace. She continued daily to lay her six children in God's hands.

With hardly any healthy young men left, the factories needed workers, and we students had to work during our holidays. We had to wash the recycled bottles for vinegar, cut the cabbage for sauerkraut and put the pickles into jars. During the summer I had to help on a farm. Being a city girl who was used to getting a suntan on the beach, I took my shorts and sunsuit along. The farmer asked me, "Is this what you want to wear in the fields?"

Not knowing what was waiting for me, I said, "Yes, I'd like to get a suntan."

"OK," he said with a smile.

First I took the basket with the big, fresh, country bread sandwiches and coffee to the field workers. I watched them picking up the grain stacks and throwing them up on the wagon. The farmer's son stacked them to each side. "May I help you do that?" I shouted.

"Sure," he said. He stopped the slow walking horses and I climbed up. From watching him I thought I knew what to do. I tried to keep up with him, at the same time getting my all-around suntan.

At the dinner table a few hours later the farmer's wife looked at me, not hiding her concern. "Are you all right?"

"Yes," I said. "A little burned, and the straw pricked me quite a bit."

She looked at the welted, beet-red skin of my legs and arms. "You can help me tomorrow with kitchen work," she said wisely.

I was glad the next morning to sit outside on a stool in the shade of the barn, peeling potatoes. Suddenly something pushed me from behind and I flew over the bucket. Looking behind me, I discovered the goat ram, peacefully chewing a potato he had stolen out of my pail.

Coming home after four weeks, I shared my first exciting farm experiences with my mother and father. Our house was quite empty, for my oldest sister, Ruth, was trained as a Red Cross nurse on a hospital ship, and my other sisters, Anneliese and Edith, were each in charge of a kindergarten. Because of this, my parents offered to take in several refugees, and it was arranged through our church. In our peaceful garden and woods these people gained new strength and hope. I wondered when this war would ever come to an end.

---

I was so grateful we still had our church life. A number of refugees from Russia, whom we called Black Sea or Bass Arabian Germans, were now attending our services. Their singing was beautiful, though we saw the signs of past strain on their faces.

One song kept going through my mind—
*Wenn Truebsahlshitze mich erschuettert.* Freely
translated it says:

> When trials' heat shall shake me deeply,
> My God Himself blows in the flames:
> In every thread my heart is shivering,
> While walking on the suffering lanes.
> But I speak softly: As God will,
> And in the fiery test I'm holding still.
> I will not murmur or complain.
> My Jesus brings me through the night;
> The end may come for me tomorrow,
> When God completes His work in me.
> He leads through trials of affliction
> To His own glorious praise alone,
> To stamp on me the seal as servant,
> I am and stay His very own,
> But I speak softly: As God will . . .

*Oh, to have that faith, that trust to be in God's
will!* I thought. *What peace is on their faces!*
I was asked to join our young people's
group and to became the pianist for our
youth choir. With all our young men being
drafted into the war, each young person was
given the names of three to five of them to
write to wherever they were stationed. We
shared with them what was going on back
home, about everyday life and church activities, and assured them that we held them up

in prayer, encouraging them in this wide-spread war. I remember writing to soldiers in Finland, Romania and France. Often the answers came weeks later from a different location, due to frequent transfers.

A number of believing soldiers who were stationed in Danzig attended our services and young people's group. As they confessed to us their spiritual needs and their homesickness, it helped us know how to encourage the soldiers to whom we were writing. After sharing our needs, we had a time of meditation. At last we stood together in a wide circle, holding hands and praying by name for each brother who was called into the war. Our service ended with a song of prayer, *Vater sieh auf unsre Brueder.* Three of the verses are as follows:

Father, look down on our brothers
From Your throne of gracious mercy
Where they are in trials today;
Keep them, Lord, from shame, despairing,
Save them out of all their bondage,
Be their help and be their peace.

When their enemies are attacking,
Strengthen, Lord, their feeble faith.
Be their hope and patience always,
Draw them to your loving heart.
Take away the pains when wounded,
As you carried all their sins.

With your precious Word give comfort;
Be their light in darkest night.
Fill them with your Holy Spirit,
Hear their longing there in secret,
Let them see what You have promised,
While You still their silent tears.

———————

Graduation from high school drew near. I came down with a very bad cold but tried not to miss my examinations. As I walked every day through the cold winter air, a sinus and ear infection set in. I tried to hide the pains until they became unbearable, and I was sent to the hospital for a serious mastoid operation on my left ear and surgery on my sinuses. Because of Mama's bad health, she was unable to visit me. I spent many lonely hours in bed with my head in a cast.

But one day my Aunt Mary came to visit me, and she carefully brought the news that my twenty-year-old brother Karl was missing in action. As a pilot of a fighter plane he was involved in air battle against the bomber planes over western Germany and did not return to his air base.

In horrible physical pain, I could not turn my head, and tears were flowing freely down my cheeks. I was hardly able to talk to explain my pain and sorrow. Yet I will never forget the love of one young nurse on the night shift who sat at my bedside gently wiping away my tears and speaking words of comfort. I believe she must have been a Christian, but I could not ask her.

———⟨≈≈≈≈⟩———

Graduation time came, and although I could not go back to school, my average marks earned me my graduation papers. After my recovery, I had to go to the employment center for counseling sessions. I wished to start a music career, possibly as a music teacher or pianist.

But with the war still going on and almost every woman called to work for the cause of the country, I was advised to choose a vocation that would serve the country. So I decided to follow the family trend to become a teacher, since two of my sisters worked in that profession and already had their own kindergarten schools, funded through the government.

A few months later I entered Kindergarten Teachers' College, a stately white villa located in my beloved woods, only a twenty-minute walk away from my home. I was to live there with twelve other girls, who had come from various parts of the country.

On my first day at the school, my mother went to sign the registration papers while I was sent to the dining room to wait for the director to take me to my class. I looked around that large room with the high ceiling, crystal chandeliers hanging between carved woodwork and a long dining table covered with white damask tablecloths. My eyes wandered along the wall, adorned with expensive wood paneling and white candle-like chandeliers—and stopped at a beautiful piano. Drawn like a magnet, I sat down and softly started to play the "Impromptu in A Flat" by Franz Shubert. Beneath the hills outside the window was a soft glistening pond in the lawn, and I forgot everything around me. *Oh, what a place to live and study for two years!* I thought. When I finished the piece, I noticed my mother with the director, Fraulein Hoffman, standing in the back of the room.

I apologized for using the instrument without asking permission.

"That is fine," Miss Hoffman said. "I am glad we have a musician among us."

I enjoyed my studies, the crafts and practical teaching, but I was most happy when I was asked to take part in the music education, playing the accordion for the folk dances we had to learn and being in charge of the preparation of a mini opera by Mozart, *Bastian and Bastien,* for a special occasion. Again I realized that all these opportunities were a sign of God's approval of my exercising my gift of music. It also seemed that God wanted to keep me out of some subjects He did not want for me—including Nazi history. Since the practicing of individual voices fell mostly on the last school hour when the Nazi history lessons were taught, the teacher told me disapprovingly that I might fail the subject. She mentioned this to Miss Hoffman, the director, who replied, "Just let that be my concern."

<center>~~~~~~~</center>

One Sunday evening I was lying on the upper bunk in our sleeping and living quarters, thinking I was all alone. I had started to read my Bible when I heard a noise in the back of the room.

I called out, "Is somebody in the room?"

"Yes, me, Elfriede."

"Oh," I said. "What are you doing?"

"I am reading," was her reply.

"What are you reading?" I wanted to know.

There was a pause. "I don't think you are interested."

"Maybe I am," I said. "I am reading too."

"What are you reading?" she asked carefully.

"I am reading my Bible."

"So am I!" she said. As if on a command, we both sat up and looked at each other.

"You are a Christian!" I said.

"Yes, I am. I am a Mennonite."

"And I am a Baptist," I replied. We just looked at each other with joy. We knew we were one in Jesus Christ. What a beautiful thing to find among the few students one who was in the same Spirit as I!

I was still able to go on with my piano studies with my piano teacher, Fraulein Krey. Often we played duets together for one or two hours on her two grand pianos. My heart was lifted up. I thought, *Music is everything! How beautiful that God made music!* My parents had bought me a secondhand grand piano, on which I loved to practice during the short times I was allowed to go home.

I was asked to be the piano accompanist for our area supervisor, who was an excellent violinist. Together with a cellist, we performed some small dinner concerts for army officers in our City Hall auditorium. I had little time to visit my parents.

There was more and more political tension in the air. The front line of the East drew closer. Many battles had been lost there on the Russian front. We, together with other students, were ordered to appear at the airport at 7 o'clock on Sunday morning to help dig the deep *pantzer Graben*, which were ditches designed to keep the tanks from coming onto the airfield. They were also designed to keep the tanks of the Russians from the east side of the city.

Miles of ditches had to be dug. We were given spades, and under supervision of some soldiers, we started digging. Around 11 o'clock I thought about my parents and church family together in the morning service, worshiping the Lord. I knew they were praying for me. One thought comforted me: I was doing something to protect our city from the immediate attacks, while our brothers had been there on the front line for years, in loneliness, cold, hardship, pain and uncertainty. Even though it was a Sunday, I was grateful that I could be here to do my duty, just as our men were ordered to do theirs. Before 2 o'clock in the afternoon we were released, and other groups came marching in to take over the work. As I remember, they worked day and night for about three weeks on that defense program. We were ordered to work there for only two more Sundays.

The Advent season started, and I was asked to play at our large sports arena for what they called a "Yuletide Hour"—Christmas songs. *I would love to do that!* I thought.

A few hundred women had gathered there for this hour. Since I knew all the melodies by heart, I could play them easily without any music. For relaxation I had chosen to play first from "The Childhood Scenes" by Robert Schuman, and some other classical pieces.

Then I looked at the program and the titles of the song sheet. *Oh, I know all these songs,* I thought. Then I realized that the word sheet on

the piano had different words. I was shocked—
these were not the old precious words I knew
from childhood. Wherever the name of Jesus
and the true message of Christmas had been,
they had put in a different meaning! I felt almost like a traitor and was angry in my heart
for being deceived, playing at this man-made
Christmas celebration where not a word of the
love of God's gift, Jesus Christ, was mentioned.
While I played these beautiful, familiar melodies, I inwardly sang the old original words in
all the songs as given by God's Holy Spirit to
His children.

*Stille Nacht, Heilige Nacht*
All is calm, All is bright
'Round yon virgin, mother and child
Holy infant so tender and mild
Sleep in heavenly peace.

Never had I sung with so much conviction
the last line of this beautiful song, "Christ the
Savior is born, Christ the Savior is born." Only
my Lord heard me.

At home later that evening, Mama told me
that something similar had happened to my
Aunt Frieda, who had a beautiful voice and
had been asked to sing at one of the first political women's meetings. She went to the front
and sang: "Jesus my pride and deepest rest . . . I
always will be in His service, of the King who

sovereignly loves me . . . I long with my heart
to see Him, His eternal kingdom to bring."

The women who had expected to hear the
*Fuehrer* lifted up were apparently stunned. But
Aunt Frieda was glad to stand up for her Lord.
Because she was well-known in her town and
the widow of the postmaster, she got away
with it, but she was never again asked to sing at
a political gathering of this new government.

We started Christmas vacation, and I was
glad to be home. We had a guest, Irmtraut, the
girlfriend of my oldest sister, Ruth, who could
not come for Christmas. The long table was set
as always, but it looked very empty. On it were
only a few gifts and a plate with homemade
cookies. I remember a pencil, a pen, an eraser
and some toothpaste—very rare articles at this
time, as a result of more than five years of war.
But then Irmtraut came to me with a little package. "Here," she said. "Maybe you can make
yourself a dirndl skirt. It will not take long and
these rags won't be used anymore."

Somewhat puzzled, I looked at the red fabric.
*Wow*, I thought. *I'll get a new skirt out of this!*
With a white blouse and dark vest, it would
look great.

Then it dawned on me. This was what was
left of a torn-up Nazi flag. Irmtraut, a National
Socialistic Party (NS) nurse, who had often
tried to argue her party's doctrines, had turned
from her misguided point of view and was

now ready to accept the Lord as her Savior. But I knew I would never put that red material around my body, regardless of how tempting it looked to me.

The most exciting gift given to me by my parents that Christmas was organ lessons with a teacher in our suburban area. Oh, how grateful I was! I could hardly wait till February when I would be back for my training as a nurse's helper at the women's clinic about seventy-five kilometers away from home.

New Year's Eve came, and we spent this night as usual in our Baptist church. We all got down on our knees fifteen minutes before the last moments of the year 1944 and continued praying into the new year of 1945, which lay before us, clouded with great uncertainty.

Without any human hope, would this long war ever come to an end? Only God's grace and mercy would carry us through the unknown year.

CHAPTER 4

---

# *Only God Knows . . .*

*I will never leave thee, nor forsake thee.*
*(Hebrews 13:5)*

*Lo, I am with you alway, even unto the end*
*of the world. (Matthew 28:20)*

The 10th of January, when I had to leave for my practical teacher training, came quickly. I had packed all my white uniforms, one Sunday dress and two or three everyday outfits (for my days off).

I was excited to be assigned a training job I had never done before—looking after newborn babies. The fact that my sister Anneliese had her kindergarten in the nearby town, just two or three kilometers' walk away, was also exciting. It would give me a chance to visit her on my day off.

At the clinic, I was welcomed by Frau Gertrud, the director and main midwife, and led to a small room, which I had all for myself. About twenty mothers, wives of high-ranking army officers, were patients there. Some had their sweet babies already, while others, still pregnant, waited for the exciting day to come. Two other midwives, NS nurses, worked with the patients. I was to observe during most of the first week.

The second week I was allowed to bathe, change and feed these sweet little darlings. Food at the dinner table was scarce for me because my ration card allowed for only the most necessary food, while the mothers had a little more. There was no table prayer said, but I still bowed my head in thanksgiving, realizing that I was often watched by patients.

I was free to visit Anneliese on Sunday. As I walked down to the village through the cold, crisp, sunny morning, the hammering of a woodpecker echoed through the woods. The trees and bushes gleamed frosty white. *How beautiful, how peaceful!* I thought. The two of us planned that the next Sunday, the 28th, which was her birthday, she would have some friends come over and we would make some music. I looked forward eagerly to that.

During the night of the 24th, I was awakened

by some distant rumbling that sounded like thunder. Still half asleep, I heard the thundering off and on. But then a loud, shrill bell rang through the house, and a hard pounding came at my door. Someone shouted, "Everybody get dressed. We evacuate within two hours. A bus is to pick us up. No one is to leave the building."

I packed my few belongings as I sat on my bedside, trying to sort out my thoughts. What could I do? My parents had no phone, nor had Anneliese—they were available only for offices or stores at that time. I knew that at home we would go down on our knees and commit our lives into God's hands. I sat there on my bed and took my little Bible out of my purse. I read a psalm and dropped to my knees, asking the Lord Jesus to be with me.

When I walked out into the hall, I was ordered to help carry some blankets, pillows and some luggage downstairs. Coming up again, I heard a mother's loud cry from labor pains, and it made me shiver. Frau Gertrud was assisting her in the operating room. Soon, through the open door, we heard the lively baby scream, and an hour later this mother was helped down the stairs to the waiting bus. In the confusion, with the mothers and newborn babies needing all our attention, I didn't want to ask again if I could leave to go to my sister. I had been told that the call from the army headquarters had commanded us to leave immediately, because the area around Danzig was already under heavy cannon fire from the Russians.

Hoping that this was just a temporary evacuation, we left in an overloaded bus at 7 a.m., trying to get around refugees and horse wagons that crowded the roads. We did not stop until 7 p.m. for a temporary overnight stay in an elementary school building in a small town. Some people there were expecting us and helped the mothers and babies. The family in the house behind the school had offered space in their home for someone to stay overnight, so Frau Gertrud sent me over.

I knocked at the door. Two friendly, elderly ladies opened the door and, seemingly expecting me, smiled. "Come in, dear. You look so tired."

My eyes fell on a meditation calendar on the wall, the same we used daily at home. "I know this calendar," I said. "We use it in our house every day."

"You are a Christian?" they asked excitedly.

"Yes," I said. "And my parents do not know where I am. I could not notify them."

"We will pray for you," they assured me.

After a cup of hot tea and a sandwich, I fell, relaxed and at peace, into the soft feather bed. *Oh, thank You, Lord, for letting me stay with these dear people.*

The next morning we were transported to a train. It had been damaged by bomb attacks and had been sidetracked. Most of the glass in the windows was shattered, but in the rush of evacuation, these trains were used. We were directed to a first-class wagon, which had upholstered seats. The mothers with babies were put in the middle. I, as temporary personnel, was advised to sit right next to the window. We attached one of the blankets we had brought to the window panes to keep out the bitter cold wind. The seat had been covered with snow that had built up a thick, icy crust. I tried to get some of it off, but people squeezed in and luggage was packed between the benches, forcing us to sit with our legs on top of it. Mothers tried to comfort their screaming babies.

We waited for hours in that situation till the train started to move. For a while I thought we might have traveled beyond the dangerous area, maybe close to the Baltic Sea. After about an hour the train stood still and again we waited for hours. Finally we moved forward again, but not for long. Then I felt the motion of going backward for a little while, and we came again to a halt.

This went on for days and nights. A little distance forward, then waiting for hours, then backward again—over and over. The seat under me gradually thawed out, and the water soaked through my coat. I was given a little piece of bacon and cheese once a day.

When the engine was moving, the mothers

may have had some hot water, for I heard them trying to figure out how to wash the dirty diapers. One night I heard a mother's half-subdued scream as she gave birth to her child, and another night soft crying as a little one died. *Oh, God,* I thought, *how long will this last?* Since it was either pitch-dark around us or almost dark because of blankets on the windows, we could see hardly anything, and only dim flashlights were used for emergency calls of mothers. No one paid any attention to me except for exchanging the most necessary words: "Could you empty this potty out the window?" or "Will you lift the blanket and see if we are near any city?"

Though there were three people sitting in this corner there was no other conversation. Everyone was occupied with her own thoughts. I wished that I could stand up—just once!—but a pile of luggage separated us from the mothers in the middle of the compartment. They at least had access to the washroom. But we had so little food and moisture intake that our needs were minimal.

With lots of snow covering the ground, most of the time I saw nothing. It kept on snowing. I caught some with my hands to get some moisture into my mouth.

It was the fourth night, and we had been standing still for hours again. My legs were cold and hurting. The position I was sitting in was at times unbearable, but except for giving my body a little change of position to relieve pressure points, I could not move from my seat. The two NS nurses were quite harsh with everyone. No one said anything of importance; there was no news that could give any hope or information about what happened on the front line, which could be anywhere close to us.

*How far are we from Danzig? Does anyone know that this train is even standing here?* I wondered. I moved the blanket to the side. It was a crisp, clear night, absolutely still, with a beautiful, crystal-clear starry sky above me. *Oh, God,* I prayed, *Your Word says that You created the heavens and that You call all the stars by name, but do You know that we are here? Do You know about me, that I am here in this darkness? I have given my life to You—do You remember me? Are You truly real? Then let me know, prove Yourself to me.*

Holding my breath, I waited in silence. . . . Then He answered me. "I will never leave you nor forsake you. Lo, I am with you always— even until the end of the earth."

A deep peace flooded my soul. It was as if I was wrapped in the arms of my heavenly Father. His presence was so real that tears of deep, inner joy ran down my face. *Oh, God! I cried inside. I love You so! Lord Jesus, You are here with me.*

He also brought to my mind the words of a song by Johann Sebastian Bach, which my mother had often sung at home while I accompanied her. *Gott lebet noch!* God is still alive! How I clung to these comforting words, recalling them over and over again:

> God is alive, oh, my soul!
> Will you despair?
> God is good, who in His mercy
> Does great things here on this earth;
> Who with mighty arms of power,
> Brings you through the darkest night.
> God can, more than we are thinking,
> Turn all things to our best.
> Oh, my soul! Remember this,
> Our God is still alive.
>
> God is alive, oh, my soul!
> Will you despair?
> So if heaven and earth may perish,
> If hell's fire seems to blow,
> Bitter enemies around you,
> Death and devil fiercely glow,
> He who trusts God, He will cover,
> And He brings them faithful through.
> Oh, my soul! Remember this,
> Our God is still alive.

Oh, how I wished to share this with all the others who sat in the almost dark train. Would anyone know and call on God as I did? Huddling there in the dark, knowing

God's presence was with me, I let my thoughts wander back home to the good times I could remember. These were the memories I would always recall and cherish in my heart: the Sunday dinners when we sang a song of thanksgiving or a canon, mostly a psalm; Mama's beautiful soprano, Papa's deep bass and we six children, automatically a double quartet; many evenings with guests coming to our home, all of us singing and singing, especially in the Advent season. Would I ever have a chance to play the piano again? Would I ever see my parents again, my beloved home, my grand piano?

———

I still had my God. He was with me all the time—and always would be. God was still alive and in me. Though I may have lost everything, I still had Him. No one could take Him out of my heart. Peacefully I fell asleep in my cramped position.

Morning came on the sixth day—Tuesday, January 30. The train had moved for awhile but had come to a halt again. I was allowed to get out of my position, climb over the luggage on the floor and go outside. How good it was to stretch for the first time and to be in an upright position! We were at a small train station out in the country.

The clean, fresh, waist-high snow glistened

under a blue sky in the bright morning sun. It
tasted so good! I melted handful after handful
in my mouth, for I had had nothing to drink
since we entered the train. There was a hopeful
joy in my heart.

Frau Gertrud, the director, called me.
"Fraulein Krüger, can you help?"

I went to support one of the mothers stepping down the steps of the train. I remembered
the gentle face of this fine lady who was the
wife of a major. She stopped every few steps,
taking a deep breath and waiting a little while,
obviously in heavy labor pains, while we led
her to the little station.

It was warm inside, and on the potbellied
stove a large pot of water told me that the
friendly officer of the station had been informed about what could happen any minute,
if everything went well with this mother.

I realized that Frau Gertrud, who had her
medical bag with her, hoped to deliver the
child right there. The labor pains had eased for
awhile. We waited. The men handed us cups of
hot tea. For me, it was the first hot drink in five
days. But then the train whistle sounded, and
the call came: "Everybody get in." Frau Gertrud
hesitated, and the forty-year-old, first-time
mother looked at her in despair, wanting to
come with us. One of the men said kindly, "We
will take care of her. My wife is at home."

Quickly I took her hand. "I will pray for you.

God will be with you. Trust Him! You will be helped."

She looked at me as if someone had given her a gift. A faint smile was on her face. "Thank you," she said.

We hurried over to the train, back to the others. My heart was heavy, and I prayed often for this brave, noble mother we had to leave behind. The driving back and forth and waiting for hours continued in the coming days and nights. Once we came to the station in a larger city, and as I looked from behind my blanket, someone from the Red Cross came to the window and handed me a cup of hot beef broth. How delicious that was! "Where are we?" I asked.

"This is Stettin," she answered. "Where do you come from?"

"We left from near Danzig on the 25th of January. I don't know how far we are going. Do you know if we will be staying here?"

She shrugged her shoulders. "Nobody knows what is going on." But I had my inner peace and deep assurance that the Lord was right with me. I felt as I had when I was a child, walking under my father's rain cape. I could not see the way, but I held his hand, knowing that he was taking me home. "He that dwelleth in the secret place of the most High shall abide under the shadow of the Almighty. . . . He shall cover thee with his feathers, and under his wings shalt thou trust" (Psalm 91:1, 4). Whatever would come, I could trust Him. He was aware of my situation.

During the long dark nights, I allowed my thoughts to wander home more and more often; recalling the memories of my childhood seemed to build a bridge to my loved ones. Soon it would be my mother's birthday. She always invited some of the poor women from our church, and they enjoyed the coffee, *kuchen* and fellowship in our home.

I remembered the best gift I ever made for her, a small embroidered tablecloth. Only ten years old, I had asked for a *Gulden,* about two marks' worth. "Mama," I said, "I have to get something very important for you."

Mama was always very wise, probably guessing from the look in my eyes that her youngest had planned a surprise. To my astonishment she asked no further questions and trusted that amount into my hand. Having worked every day after school on that embroidery, I presented it proudly on her birthday. How her beautiful dark eyes lit up! Her expression of surprise and thankful joy was for me the greatest reward. Remembering her, a flood of fearful worry about her wanted to creep into my heart. I prayed in faith, *Oh, Lord, You are also there with her.*

Oh, it was so good, so comforting, to have memories.

On February 5, the twelfth day of our journey, we arrived at our destination and were told to leave the train. We were in Parchim, a small town near Mecklenburg, in North Germany. We had covered about 350 kilometers. Together with another small private clinic, we were placed in a castle called *Schloss Mentin*, which served as an emergency center. We had our first meal at a table, with bread and some lunch meat, yet there was an atmosphere of grief and pain.

I saw the exhausted faces of the mothers and realized that some of their babies were no longer with them. I felt sick and numb inside, unable to speak any words of comfort.

Frau Gertrud pulled me aside. "Fraulein Krüger, I'd like you to sleep with me in the room they assigned for me." Whispering, she added, "I do not trust these two NS nurses. I have some of my valuables with me. Come with me."

There was only one bed in the room. We would fit in together. At least we could lie down and stretch out.

Oh, how wonderful that felt after sitting for twelve days and nights in a crunched-up position, my legs falling asleep, trying to get a little warm when the train was moving and heat came through the pipes! Here we even had clean sheets on the bed and real pillows.

Frau Gertrud showed me a suitcase with

beautiful silverware and some lovely jewelry. "Would you mind watching over this? You are so different from the others. You seem to be so at peace. Why is it?"

We were already tucked into our bed.

"Oh," I said, "I have a strong faith in God. I gave my life to Him; I'm a Christian."

"I wish I could have that," she replied. "I strongly think of putting an end to my life. My husband and my three sons are on the east front line. I do not know if anyone is alive, and I don't know what I should do or where to go from here."

I prayed quietly. "God knows all about us. He told me that He will not leave me or forsake me, and I trust Him. You too can call on Him," I said. There was silence, and I fell asleep.

The next day I was called to the supervisor of this emergency setup. "Here is a letter for you which came through the government. By the way, you can think of where you want to go from here. We were notified by the officials that all nonprofessional staff can go wherever they want."

I pressed the letter to my racing heart and went into the little bathroom and locked myself in. With shaking hands I opened the letter, recognizing the handwriting of my papa. It was the seventh of February, my mother's birthday. It was like a greeting from her. Tears ran down my face, and I cried silently for a while. *Oh, God, what would I do without You!*

The letter was two weeks old. The enemy had been around the city at that time. Were they still home? I could not place them in my mind anywhere else. My thoughts wandered home to them, and through my tears I started slowly to read the letter. My heart shivered at the news. Papa had tried to reach me there, seventy-five kilometers away from home, riding his bicycle on icy roads where fragments of army groups tried to draw back and fight the enemy.

Some officers had tried to stop his journey, calling him foolish for trying to find his daughter. After many hours on the road, he arrived at the village of Pelplin and went to my sister Anneliese, who was preparing to leave with others the next day, knowing nothing about me.

He finally found the little clinic I was supposed to be in but was told by the custodian that we all had left early in the morning the same day, January 25.

He had come six hours too late. Without resting he turned his bike around and rode back to Danzig. Several times his bike slipped and he fell, bruising hips and arms on the icy roads. His knuckles bleeding, he arrived home totally exhausted, where my mother and grandparents and some homeless refugees were waiting and praying for him.

His last sentence in the letter was, "Keep lov-

ing your Savior. We have laid you in His faithful hands."

I was so homesick I could not stop crying.
*Oh, God, what happened during these last two*
*weeks? Lord, I know You are with them. But are*
*these their last words to me? Will I never see them*
*again? Lord, give me grace to be strong and trust*
*that You will keep protecting them.* My tears
gradually stopped, and I washed my eyes.
With some peace in my heart that He was with
them, I unlocked the door and went into our
bedroom and waited for Frau Gertrud. As I re-
read the letter, my thoughts wandered home to
my parents, thinking of their love for me and
the dangerous, sacrificial ride of my father to
find his youngest one.

Oh, how much they must be daily in prayer
for all of us—and me! Oh, to have always such
strong faith that had carried them through
these past years since my two brothers were reported missing!

Frau Gertrud came to call me for dinner, so I
told her the news I heard from the supervisor.
She thought for a while. "There is no way for
you or me to get back," she said.

"I will try to find my sister-in-law in Heuholz
near Oehringen, in South Germany," I replied.
"She is the wife of my older brother, who is
missing. Maybe I can stay there."

"I am supposed to get seventy-five marks for
the train," the supervisor said. Leaning close to

me, she whispered, "I was thinking it over last night. I will come with you to the train station. I will not stay with these Nazis. I'll find a way."

I washed the clothes I had worn for twelve days on the train and packed up. After dinner Frau Gertrud had made arrangements for the coachman of the house to take me to the railroad station in the evening so I could take an early morning train down south—the only direction one *could* go, for we were sandwiched in between two front lines, the East and the West.

While I was putting my little suitcase together, she packed hers, too. She explained, "I told the man to pick me up at the other back door. I'll come right with you."

No one noticed that we left. We slept on the bench in the little waiting room of the small station. In the morning my train came. She hugged me and said, "I will go to a relative of mine till everything is over. Thank you for giving me new hope and faith in God again."

CHAPTER 5

# *Enough Bullets for All of Us*

*I will instruct thee and teach thee in the way which thou shalt go: I will guide thee with mine eye. (Psalm 32:8)*

The train was loaded with people. Like bees on a beehive, they clung to anything they could hold onto, sitting on the roof and in between the wagons. How would I get on?

*Help me, Lord*, I prayed.

Someone said, "Young lady, you can't get in through the door."

Some soldiers opened the window and shouted, "Come here."

Someone lifted me up and they pulled me through the window. I found a place for my feet on the floor among all the luggage and people.

"See, there's lots of room," they said, laughing.
The train started rolling.

*Lord, thank You,* I said in my heart. *Is this what I should do—go down to South Germany where my sister-in-law lives?*

After a while I pulled my little notebook out of my pocket. Standing close to the window, I wanted to read some Bible verses I had written down. While looking through it, I noticed an address on the back cover of the booklet:

Bruno Krüger
Gommern by Magdeburg
Marketplace #2.

*This is Papa's brother,* I thought, amazed. He had visited us several years ago. I must have taken the address at that time to write him. *Lord, is that the place You want me to go instead?*

I asked someone around me if we would pass Magdeburg and if they knew if it was far to Gommern. I found out that there should be a train connection around midnight. In Magdeburg I got off the train.

There were people everywhere. An older soldier who had told me that my connection was at midnight went with me to the right platform. I got safely onto the next train and arrived in the dark, early morning hours in the little town of Gommern. Only a few other refugees like me got off. So as not to surprise and disturb my uncle, I stayed in the waiting room until the sun came up.

I felt somehow safe. Someone who would remember me lived close by. I stayed till daylight, and at 8 o'clock I left the warm little place. With my suitcase in my hand, I asked my way to Marketplace #2.

There were two names and bells on the front door. The one on the upper apartment had my last name, Krüger. Someone opened the door and looked through the small crack. A sleepy voice asked me, "Yes? What do you want?"

"I am Magdalene Krüger from Danzig. Is my Uncle Bruno here?"

"No, he is at work."

"May I come in?" I asked.

The small but sturdy woman in a housecoat opened the door a little wider.

"Yes," she replied.

I followed her to the upper apartment. She called, "Hilde! Hannelore! Get up! We have a visitor!"

My cousins came out of their bedrooms, looking me over, up and down. I looked like one of the refugees.

When my uncle came home from the office at the shoe factory, he took me into his arms. "So, this is the little Magda I remember from when I visited my brother!"

*Oh,* I thought, *it feels so good to be hugged!*

"You look so much like my father," I said.

Even his voice sounded like his. My cousin Hannelore, who was sixteen, had to share her room with me. I could sleep on the upper bunk. Tante Helene, my uncle's wife, was not very happy about my stay.

Every day more refugees streamed through the little town. Schools and halls became shelters for them. My aunt took me to the food distribution center. After standing in line for a long while, I was interviewed and identified as a refugee and I received my food ration card.

"You are lucky," she said, "that you can stay with us. You could have been put in one of these places with all the others."

I said that I was very thankful.

As the days went by, I noticed more and more that my presence was not welcome. One morning while I was reading my New Testament, still lying in bed, Aunt Helene came in to wake up Hannelore.

"What are you reading?" she asked.

"My New Testament," I answered.

Annoyed, she looked at me. "You know you should not read that."

"Why?" I asked. "I was brought up with the Bible. It is God's Word that gave me strength and hope in these hard days. Have you never read it?"

Angrily she cut me off. "I could report you, reading the Jewish book. They might discontinue your food ration card."

I held on to the precious book. I was afraid that in the future she would take it away from me.

Through conversations within that family I realized that they all belonged to the Nazi Party. Though my uncle was not a Nazi at heart, because of his position as manager in the shoe factory he was forced to join it.

Spring came early in middle Germany's mild temperatures, and so came Easter. Uncle Bruno started to work in his back yard, and I loved to help him. Being with him made me feel comfortable and somewhat secure. The bond of family relationship was there. I thought much of home, where I used to help my father in the garden, getting the dry leaves from under the bushes. I had developed a great love for garden work and told Uncle Bruno about our backyard.

"Oh, yes, I remember," he said. "Your property was very beautiful. Your mother was quite a gardener. She kept it looking like a jewel box."

On the next Sunday morning he went down to the garden and I went with him again. When I was alone with him, I asked, "Are we not going to church?"

He answered, "I know you people do that, but I can think of God here in nature. He is in my garden, too, as He is with you in the church."

I didn't know what to say to that.

I had become good friends with their dog, an Irish setter, sometimes taking him for a walk with Hannelore to see her grandma. With Hannelore I could sometimes share a little at night before we went to sleep, asking her if she knew any of the songs I knew from back home, like some lullabies and some evening songs. She could not understand my enthusiasm, for their family life was entirely different from ours. But still, to comfort my own heart, I sang for her in my upper bunk bed some of the beautiful songs we sang at home, about God's creation, the evening tide and the joyful morning songs my mother sometimes woke us up with. One especially dear to my heart was *Frueh morgens eh' die haehne kraehn*:

> Early before the rooster crows,
> Before the birds begin to sing,
> When softly from high mountaintop,
> An echo through the valley rang,
> Walk softly, oh, so softly,
> Our loving God through fields and woods.
>
> The brook, which knows He is coming near,
> Will stop its rushing sound at once,
> And not disturb this holy time,
> Of praise and worship on the earth,
> And all the trees will bow their heads,
> Because the Lord walks through the woods.

"We do not sing in our house," Hannelore said. "My mother never sings. I do not think she can."

I felt sadness in my heart and compassion for her. Our relationship was a little closer then and we walked the dog together a few times.

---

Good Friday came, and once more I shyly approached my uncle when he was downstairs in the garden.

"Are we going to church today? It is Good Friday!"

I thought that on this still-official holiday everybody would go, especially since the radio reported cities fallen in the battles close to us, and fear and hopelessness were all around us.

"Why don't you go by yourself? There is a Lutheran church a few blocks away," he replied.

I went to the church with the high, slim steeple and entered through the main door. The inside auditorium was half-lit. The beautiful, stained-glass windows gave only a dim light. I thought to myself, *I came too early.* Just as I wanted to sit down to take the stillness in, I noticed someone in the back of the church—an old woman sitting on the last bench, a kerchief over her head.

Softly I asked, "When does the service start?"

She motioned with her hand toward the front. I looked at the elevated pulpit and noticed a man in a dark robe entering. It must have been the pastor. He opened the big Bible and very softly mumbled a few words. I couldn't understand a word he said and he left again.

I sat there. Was it a prayer? Was it God's Word? I was waiting to see what would come then, but nothing happened. No organ playing, no people, no message. Totally aghast, I turned to the old woman. She shrugged her shoulders as if to say, "That is all. Nothing more."

It was like a dream. *It can't be. What is happening to us? Does no one remember that this is Good Friday, the day Jesus died on the cross for our sins?* My thoughts were turning around and around. I felt like going to the marketplace and shouting, "Listen, people! Remember this is a great day when Jesus took our sins on Himself. Without this we are all lost in these hopeless days!"

There was no one to share with, no one to pray with, no one who would understand. I went back to my uncle's place. He was not in the garden anymore, but the dog was lying at the garden house. I went upstairs and asked if I could take the dog for a walk.

My aunt said with a mocking laughter, "Oh, church is already done, eh?"

I took the dog and walked to the outskirts of the town, and on a little hill on a dry heather patch I sat down. Holding onto the dog and burying my face in his soft fur, I cried. I was so lonely, so very sad inside. *What has my country come to?*

A little sun came through the clouds, and the dog licked my hand. He seemed to understand my pain. Gradually my tears stopped and my mind wandered home again to Danzig. *All those at home are one with me in spirit,* I thought. *Even these many hundred kilometers cannot separate us. The Lord Jesus who died for our sins also rose for us at Easter in victory. Over all this darkness we will be together in eternity with Him, regardless what happens to all of us.* Peace and joy filled my heart again.

As I entered the house, my inner strength was restored for my Lord was with me. Easter dinner ended, and we even had a piece of cake.

Aunt Helene said, "You know, Bruno, if they don't get this new weapon finished, soon we will be all finished, for there is nowhere to go. I hope you know what you have to do."

"Yes, I know," he answered.

"What do you mean, Uncle?" I asked.

"Well," he replied, "we will end up right here. Don't worry. I have enough bullets—there is one for you."

"Uncle Bruno," I said, hardly believing my ears, "you will not do that. Why don't you trust God? He can protect you all too. He has been with me. Why don't you believe in Him?"

My aunt dismissed me with a wave. "Nonsense," she said.

Uncle Bruno spoke again. "I know your father has a strong faith, but I have the responsibility for you. I cannot leave you behind when the Russians take over."

Deeply disturbed about the complete unbelief of this family, I sat down to write a letter to my parents. Whether it reached them or not, I had to talk to them. Yet I would not mention the bullet at all. I knew the Lord was with me. He would not leave me or forsake me.

---

It was on the following Tuesday that a bomb attack on Magdeburg, just a few kilometers away from us, was announced. We went into the little shelter. Soon the sirens sounded the end of the air raid, and we went to bed. The window of our bedroom was open. It was a mild evening and I heard the amsel, the early bird of spring. My thoughts went back home. Oh, how often my mama called us, "Come hear the amsel sing." The bird sat on the highest branch of the tall birch tree, singing her beautiful evening song. I wonder if Mama is still . . . My thoughts stopped. It was now two-and-a-half months since I had left home. It must be spring there too. The little blue flowers under the hazelnut tree near the *laube* must be out. *Oh, God, You are everywhere. Your seasons never end. You make everything new again on earth.*

Almost asleep, I suddenly heard a voice calling, "Hello? Is there a family Krüger living here?"

I sat up. I knew that voice! It was the voice of my sister Edith.

I was out of the room and down the stairs in one move. I ripped the front door open, and Edith and I collapsed in each other's arms as if we would never let go again.

She had left Danzig just a few days ago. Mama and Papa were still OK, wanting to stay with our grandparents and our Aunt Lydia. The father of Edith's girlfriend, who was in charge of the evacuation, got her and his daughter and wife over the Baltic Sea with one of the last ships leaving Danzig. Even so, the ship *Wilhelm Gustloff* did not make it, and just a few days before, thousands had met a tragic death in the icy waters of the Baltic Sea.

Edith had brought a suitcase with my clothes and some of my favorite jewelry—an amber necklace Fraulein Fischbeck had given me and a silver necklace with an amber pendant, the first prize in a contest for knowing the most names for Jesus Christ. She also brought with her my wooden letter box and writing pen with engraved, burned-in flowers my father had given me some years ago, part of the whole desk set I loved so much. Even my black concert dress was in the suitcase. All these precious pieces from home had been packed by my mama's own hands in faith, wondering if these things would ever reach me. I knew that many tears and prayers went with them.

Papa had advised Edith to look for me first at my cousin Karl's home in Celle, near Hanover. Hearing from his widowed wife, Gertrud, that I had found shelter with Uncle Bruno in Gommern, she left her suitcase with her kindergarten materials in Celle. Instead she brought my suitcase so I could have some greetings from home. She also shared how she had fled with some farmers on a horse-pulled wagon train, leaving her kindergarten, about 150 kilometers south of Danzig, and everything else behind. They drove for days through heavy snow, crossing over the Weichsel (Vistula) River. Several wagons loaded with families broke through the ice and never made it. It was a miracle that she finally arrived in Danzig.

But my Aunt Helene was not very happy having another family member in her home. "How many more of these people are coming?" she asked my uncle.

"You don't know what these people have lost," he said. "They come from a very fine home."

Edith and I both felt a little uncomfortable. "I think we two should try to live on our own," she said to me when we were alone. "I can always find children to care for. And maybe everything will soon calm down."

# CHAPTER 6

# Twenty Marks
# to No Return

*No weapon that is formed against thee shall
prosper. (Isaiah 54:17)*

I felt I should go with Edith to Celle, about
one-and-a-half hours by train from Gommern, to retrieve her belongings. Nothing
would separate me from her again! Uncle
Bruno lent me twenty marks, despite my aunt's
protesting he would never get it back.

We left on the following Friday afternoon.
After we had ridden about thirty minutes on
the overcrowded train, bullets shattered the
glass of the windows. Although we had been
squished like sardines as we stood in the aisles,
we all ducked our heads. Moments later the
train came to a halt.

"Get away from the train!" someone shouted.
"It's fighter planes!"

Everyone pushed in panic toward the exit
and ran over the rough, plowed field toward
some bushes for cover. Before we could get
there, the fighter planes returned, just a few
yards above the ground, it seemed, racing toward us. "Get down!" someone yelled.

We threw ourselves onto the field. I looked
up and could clearly see the pilot and the firing
machine guns. Dirt flew around and over us.
Some people screamed; an older man was shot
in the leg and others were wounded.

Edith tried in panic to get up again, but I
held on to her leg. With urgent calmness I said,
"Let's sing, Edith. Let's die together." With an
unexplainable strength deep inside, I started to
sing, "*Wenn der Heiland als Koenig erscheint und
die Seinen als Erloeste im Himmel vereint* . . .
When He cometh, when He cometh, to make
up His jewels."

Again beautiful peace flooded my heart,
peace beyond understanding. I knew that if
He wanted us to come home, I was ready to
go.

The plane turned away, never to come back.
We heard later that the train's steam engine
was hit, and the engineer was shot in the stomach. We had to wait for another engine and engineer to continue the trip.

It was late at night before we were able to

board the train and move on. We arrived about an hour later in Celle.

We left the dim lights of the railroad station, and Edith tried to remember the way back to Gertrud's house. We stumbled down a main street, trying to read street signs in total darkness. Suddenly we were engulfed by the bright beams of a fighter plane searching the streets for anything moving. Edith and I stopped dead, pressing against a house wall. Another plane roared close by. We ran breathlessly from house to house, hiding and leaping into the dark doorways. *Lord, help us find the house!* I prayed desperately. Again a plane approached, throwing searchlights over the streets. We stopped at the street corner. . . . Something was moving in the shadow. A person? A dog?

The sound of deadly machine guns shattered the air, echoing through the street. Pressing into the shadow of a wall, we held our breath but heard nothing else. *Oh, God, let no one be hurt.* Then by the flash of a beam, Edith recognized the street sign on the corner. "We are close to Gertrud's street," she whispered. "One block more and we should be there." Exhausted, we finally found Gertrud's house. When we knocked on the door, we heard a voice that was very familiar to me.

"Who is there?"

"That is Tante Mariechen," I gasped.

Edith answered her, "It is Edith and Magda."

The door opened, and for the first time I saw Tante Gustel.

"Oh, you poor girls! Come in."

It was amazing how similar Tante Gustel's voice was to that of my Aunt Mariechen from back home in Danzig. She and Aunt Mina, Papa's sisters, had fled from Bad Freienwalde, east of Berlin, when the Russian front drew closer. They wanted to be with Gertrud, her daughter-in-law, and her three little children. Gertrud, a tall blonde, came out of her bedroom and hugged us too.

"Girls," she said, "you can sleep in one of the children's beds. I will take one of them into my bed." Oh, how good to lie down in peace!

The next morning they encouraged us to rest up over Sunday and to leave for Gommern on Monday . It was a beautiful, sunny Sunday afternoon as we walked with Gertrud toward the airport. Suddenly the sirens sounded. Some soldiers near the airport signaled us to go back, expecting an attack on the airport. We ran back toward the city limits as fast as we could. Gasping for breath, Gertrud said, "I don't expect trouble. We've never had a bomb attack on Celle during the war. A castle owned by the Mountbatten family of England is here." We settled into an easy walk. Looking up we saw the bomber bulks, like little, silver fish, in accurate formation over us in the blue sky. Getting closer to the street where Gertrud's house was, we realized two freight trains were blocking the road.

We looked up. Over us were several clusters of glistening, egg-like bombs sliding toward the trains, about 200 yards before us. Ear-bursting explosions shattered the air. Flying high were parts of the train cars and wood pieces—and people.

I saw a high factory fence to my right, but then my mind went blank. . . .

<hr/>

The next thing I remember was being in an earth bunker or fruit cellar. In the dark I heard voices.

I called frantically, "Is there an Edith Krüger here?"

"Magdchen, are you all right?" Out of the darkness I heard Edith's and Gertrud's voices.

It will be in heaven that my Lord will reveal to me how He got us over to the other side of the fence and into the cellar. Does it not say in one of His psalms, "By my God have I leaped over a wall" (Psalm 18:29)?

When the explosions stopped and we got outside, SS guards were there with their revolvers, looking for escaped concentration camp prisoners from one of the trains.

The second train carried ammunition. Over the twisted railroad tracks and smoking cars we tried to get to Gertrud's house as fast as possible. A few yards away from her home my knitted jacket lay on the sidewalk among bits of broken glass, pieces of roof shingles and other debris that had flown out of the houses.

When we reached her apartment, almost all the glass panels were gone because of the pressure of the explosions, and a part of the roof was on the ground. We did not find anyone in that apartment and ran down the basement stairs, where the children, with their grandma and aunt, were found safe. Oh, how grateful we all were that God had been with them and us, protecting us from any harm!

The railroad station was also destroyed. No train could get in or out of the town. *Does God want to keep us away from Gommern?* I wondered.

It was the following Thursday that the American tanks moved into the streets and we came under the protection of the Allies.

We were under curfew and could never leave the city. Except for two hours around noon, we could not leave the house.

I had no shoes that fit—the only pair I had, which I had gotten from Uncle Bruno, were tight and hurt me very much. Gertrud offered to take them to the shoemaker to stretch them. The next day when we went to retrieve them, the whole shoe repair shop was empty—every pair of shoes was stolen by the prisoners who roamed the streets. There I was, only my blue skirt, my blouse and my little knitted jacket to call my own—not even shoes to wear!

The two hours around noon when the curfew was lifted were the only time to go and hunt for food. Finding food for five adults and three children was quite a challenge. One of my aunts lent me her shoes to wear so I could go along.

One day we were told to go down to the army quarters of the Allies. They needed women to peel potatoes and vegetables for the English and American soldiers. Edith could go, but I had no shoes. We were told that at the city hall there were clothes and shoes for each one who didn't have any. The citizens of Celle were asked to donate clothing for the many thousands of refugees who swarmed the city. With my aunt's shoes I went to the city hall and got a pair of black suede leather shoes with high heels and a light blue pair of knee stockings. *What a combination!* I thought, but we laughed about these things, grateful that we had something to wear.

Food for all of us was getting very scarce. The shelves in the stores had been emptied, and they were now closed up. No new food supply was coming in. Gertrud was told that outside the town there was a field where we were allowed to work and put some seed in for vegetables. The hot noon sun burned down, and the ground was very dry and hard. There was no water nearby, and we did not have the right tools, only one spade and a rake for the three of us to work. Often when I straightened up after pulling the weeds which were covering the ground, everything in front of me was shiny and blurry because of malnutrition. Holding on to the spade or rake, I waited till this was over and the dizziness disappeared so I could get down and work again for a little while.

---

The war came to an end on May 5, 1945. Oh, what a release! How long we had waited for that day!

But there was no big parade, no fanfare, no celebration. A dark sorrow hung over us all. And for millions there was no word, no mail, no news about what was really going on. The front lines of the Western Allies and Russians had met and the borderline of East and West Germany was set and would stay.

What happened to the millions of torn-apart families? Would they ever come together?

There was no possible way for us to know what had happened to Uncle Bruno's family; there was no mail or other communication anywhere. I could only trust God with the whereabouts of my parents and sisters, because I was completely out of contact with them as well.

But every time I thought of them, a calm peace filled my heart.

---

I still remember the unusual sight of a battle between two fighter planes on the Sunday before the war ended. That afternoon we went down to the river, the Aller, and at the bridge people were lining the railing, looking up into the blue sky where two fighter planes chased each other. I thought of my brother, Karl, who had flown a plane like that. Who is going to win . . . the Germans or the Allies? My heart was heavy. Except for the roaring sounds of the planes of those two brave pilots, there was absolute silence among the people.

I didn't know what to think. The whole war was so senseless—and now it was coming to an end, but still we felt no release from all the pain and hurt it left behind.

The consequences of senseless destruction, killing and dying would linger on . . . oh, for how long?

The two planes had vanished in the air.

---

A church service for Protestants in *der Stadtkirche* of Celle was announced on the doors of this beautiful cathedral-like church in the middle of the city. Hundreds of people filled the benches and even the two balconies halfway around the walls.

But the message brought no blessings to my heart. The pastor talked only about the good news that the war had ended and that people would soon have a place to stay again. I waited in vain for a word of comfort as I stared at the pale, hungry faces of refugees all around me. The powerful pipe organ ended with "A Mighty Fortress Is Our God," but no one sang. People from all over shattered, broken-up Germany, hurting, choked up with tears, attending church for the first time after the war, were not able to sing.

*If only these people could be pointed to Jesus!* I thought. *Why did the pastor not tell them about the only One who could give them peace and rest?*

CHAPTER 7

# A Time of Peace

*My soul, wait thou only upon God; for my
expectation is from him. . . . Trust in him at
all times; ye people, pour out your heart before him: God is a refuge for us. Selah.
(Psalm 62:5, 8)*

As I came out of church one day, I met a
young girl walking with two older ladies. They smiled and asked if I was a resident
of Celle.

"No," I said. "I am a refugee from Danzig."

Excitedly, the girl said, "I am from Posen,
about 150 kilometers from Danzig."

We talked more and agreed to meet again.
Elfriede became my friend—she had such humor, and we had lots of fun. She was well educated in English. One of the two older ladies,
her aunts, was an English teacher and an inter-

preter for the English officials and Germans. We often spoke English together.

On my eighteenth birthday I got a little blue notebook, a treasure in a time when no writing paper was anywhere to be found. In this book I wrote as much as possible of my memories of the flight from Danzig, using it as my diary. To save lots of space for my writing, I wrote in tiny letters. With Elfriede whom I called Friedel, I went through the town that day, and we read all the beautiful inscriptions on the beams of the *Fachwerkhauses* (houses in Tudor style).

I thanked God for a friend such as this, His birthday gift to me!

---

A few days later I walked again through this beautiful city, looking at the inscriptions on the *Fachwerkhauses*, which reminded me of the many inscriptions found in the old city of Danzig. Up beside the *Stadtkirche* was a house with a brass plate at the door. It said:

Professor and Doctor H. Schmidt
Music Director and Organist

My heart beat faster. I thought of home and the organ lessons my parents had promised me. *Maybe I have a chance. Oh, God, You know that I would love so much to learn how to play that beau-*

*tiful instrument!* My hand almost automatically touched the doorbell. I waited.

From a window on the second floor a woman called, "Can I help you?"

I asked if Dr. Schmidt was there.

"No," she said.

"Oh," I said. "Does he teach the organ?"

"Well," she said, "with churches opening up again, he is about to start again as soon as he has a class together, possibly in the beginning of September."

A few weeks later I had an interview and was accepted.

September came, and together with five others, I went for my first instruction on that beautiful pipe organ, with its eighty-six stops and three manuals. J.S. Bach's picture was beside it with a framed letter verifying his approval of the organ, which he had tried out and played so many decades ago. Because of my musical background, I quickly understood the basics and was assigned some exercises with it. I tried to practice several times a week. Dr. Schmidt also told me that the Motetten Choir would start soon, and he wanted his younger organ students to attend. I would have to get some voice training. Oh, how excited I was!

Willing to do anything to get back to my beloved music, I had found a job as a nanny for Gertrud's friend, a dentist with three little boys. The home of this family was just around the block, at the park that surrounded the castle.

When Gertrud took Edith and me to meet these people, we had a cup of tea together. When the lady of the house got up to serve more tea, she looked down at Edith's feet and said with a little smile, "Excuse me, Fraulein Krüger, do you mind telling me where you got your shoes?"

"From the city hall, the donations for refugees," Edith said.

"Well, I am so glad that you got my shoes."

We all broke out in laughter. Then going to her dresser, she got Edith one of her nightgowns and me a slip, surely rare articles.

One day there was a great surprise: Our sister Anneliese arrived. With great joy we welcomed her—now three of our family were together. She had left two days after we evacuated with our little clinic and had traveled with the staff from her kindergarten. She shared with us several of her experiences, and we saw how God had faithfully kept His hand over her life too. One of the things she shared was that she would have lost her only pair of shoes to a Russian soldier if it had not been for the little four-year-old son of one of her helpers. The child had fought the soldier off, beating him with his little fists and crying, "Leave Aunt Anneliese's shoes alone!"

Gertrud's apartment got very crowded with

my two aunts still there, her own three children, Edith and I and now Anneliese. But God knew all about this too and would take care of us. My sisters had brought the news about my mother's cousin, "Uncle" Fritz Mundt, who, I discovered, also lived in Celle and had come back from the war some weeks before that. Gertrud, who had been one of his students at the business and career college where he was the principal, went with us to meet him. We recognized him immediately by his resemblance to my mother's family.

Just a few weeks later he was ordered to evacuate his beautiful villa for the occupying military officials within twenty-four hours, taking only the most necessary belongings with him. Uncle Fritz notified us about this. He owned two other apartment buildings, and he asked us girls to move into the custodian's apartment above the garages across from one of his apartment buildings so he could store some of his valuable possessions there to keep them from being confiscated by the military. At night he had some people move some of his most valuable furniture, Persian rugs, paintings, vases and other lovely things into this apartment.

Edith and I, having nothing of our own, moved gladly into these luxurious, beautiful surroundings. We felt like princesses in such a richly furnished place. How we thanked the

Lord! Uncle Fritz moved into one of his houses at the other end of town.

———

It was the end of September and the weather was beautiful. We still had no word of my older sister Ruth. In vain we had often looked through the lists, nailed to the city hall and other official buildings, of the thousands of refugees moving through our city, Celle. Inquiring at the Red Cross station, we were advised to try to get down to the Red Cross headquarters in Munich, Bavaria, in South Germany. It would be very risky trying to get from our English Zone through the French and American Zone without a permit! But we decided to take a train to the closest French Zone border.

After an hour on the train I felt sick and feverish. *Maybe when they see I'm ill, they will allow us to stay on the train past the border!* I thought. *But then again, maybe the Lord doesn't want us to go on this long, dangerous trip!* I was dizzy and knew that I couldn't go on. I prayed, *Lord, You know how I feel. Please guide us.*

We got off the train and started to walk aimlessly down a street. I felt that Edith should knock on the door of the corner house. A woman opened the door and Edith explained our situation. The woman let us use an old mattress and blanket in an empty bedroom and gave us something hot to drink.

Early in the morning she woke us up. I felt well enough to go on. We followed her directions to a nearby crossing, where we also found the large culvert leading through a dry ditch under the railroad tracks into the French Zone. At the other side was a cornfield, and from there we could see a guard walking in the distance. In this sparsely planted area, we had to crawl on our stomachs and elbows like soldiers to avoid being seen. Despite the danger of being discovered, Edith and I allowed ourselves suppressed giggles as we watched each other crawl.

Reaching the end of the field, we casually walked into a little orchard where we cleaned ourselves up as well as possible before heading to the road. Thankful that the Lord had watched over us and trusting He would guide us further, we started on our hitchhiking adventure.

At one crossing we were allowed to hide inside the large tires on a big American transporter, where the American soldiers let us go with them across the border of the French-American section. At the border we had to stop.

The doors were pulled open and other guards asked, "Anything in it?"

"Just tires," the man replied.

With long iron rods they hit and poked in between the bunches of tires. We held our breath and prayed. The rods never hit us.

Many different, difficult hurdles had to be covered during that trip. Yet I was so continually in prayer that there was not a night where the Lord did not find a house for us, where someone took us in. Once we stayed in a little village where a woman opened her home to us and gave us a room with a big feather bed, just like one at home, and a piece of country bread with sausage.

"Girls," she said, "you should not be outside this late. It's almost dark. The soldiers like pretty girls like you. I have a daughter your age in the city. I know."

Exhausted and happy that somebody cared for us, we sank into the deep feather cushions. The next morning she gave me a pair of silk stockings for the cool days to come. What a rarity! I will never forget that sweet lady.

Other times we were only allowed to sleep in the loft of a barn in a corner of straw. But we thanked the Lord for a roof over our heads.

We had come into the area where our sister-in-law, Marle, the wife of our missing brother Heinz, was living. With the help of a map Uncle Fritz had given us, we traveled through the province called *Schwabenland* near Heidelberg, full of fruit orchards and hills with wine plantations. That evening, not knowing where to sleep, we asked two young men in the village if they knew of a farmer who would let us sleep in a barn. In their Schwabisch dialect they said,

"You can sleep in the *g'mise* house." Not sure what they meant, we followed them to a greenhouse past their parents' farm. It was warm there, and we could watch the stars and the moon through the glass roof. The Lord seemed very close to us.

We found Marle and her parents totally surprised by our arrival. For each of us it was a renewing of faith and hope that one day word would come that her missing husband, our dear brother, would come home. After two days of rest and good food we moved on. In Munich we found that our sister was not registered yet, but there were still millions who had not registered in the cities, not knowing where they were going to stay. We left our address in Celle with them, and with some financial help from Marle's family we were able to start home by train, ID papers stating that we were residents of the English Zone in our hands.

The crossroads of the bigger highways were littered with homeless refugees or former German soldiers trying to find relatives. We joined one group of drifters when we discovered they were waiting to go to Ulm, where we were heading. A friendly black US soldier stopped and invited as many as could squeeze in to climb into his truck. He raced down the narrow, winding road, singing loudly and laughing at his human cargo, who were frantically holding on to whatever they could. Shaking inside and out, some of us climbed down at the next stop, hoping for a safer ride to come along.

But once more it was not home where we spent the night. This time it was in the remains of a large railroad station in Ulm. Rain dripped through the roof everywhere. But then I saw a little platform where it was dry and found an American newspaper that became our cover for the night. Newspaper can keep you pretty warm! I thought of Jacob, who slept with his head on a rock—God watched over him, and He would watch over us too.

We arrived in Celle without further difficulty.

Edith got a job in the Christian home of a count and countess, caring for their six little girls. Having worked for the Allies, washing windows, cleaning rooms, etc., with a group of other young women for awhile, she was glad to be back in her profession as kindergarten teacher.

One Sunday afternoon, walking with my friend Friedel home to our apartment up the Luneburger Strasse, I suddenly stopped, hardly believing my ears. Through a half-open window I heard the beautiful, familiar "I Need Thee Every Hour."

Pulling Friedel behind me I went through a

small garden gate to the side door and followed the sound coming through a poorly lit entranceway out of the living room. There were eight or ten people singing this song so dear to my heart. Someone offered us a chair. My eyes fell on the little pedal organ and the open songbook with numbers written over the words. I had never seen someone play from a songbook like this. But they sang from their hearts.

I felt so much at home! Now I had found a group of true believers. After that song they asked if someone had a request. Somebody called out a song but the player didn't know it.

I called from the back, "I know this song. May I play it?"

Surprised, they all looked around. A brother, noticing me, pointed to the pedal organ. "Come here," he said. "Welcome! Who are you?"

I explained, "I am a Baptist, coming from Danzig. I'm a refugee."

Tears of joy were running down my face as we sang some more songs. Then the older brother preached the gospel, the true message of God. Oh, it was like being back home! Though I had enjoyed the Motetten Choir and the cantatas under the leadership of music director Schmidt, the services in the Stadtkirche had been quite stiff and technical, and I had greatly missed the true fellowship I had in our chapel in Danzig.

This small group of faithful Christians

started slowly to grow as more refugees became aware of it. One by one God brought us together.

My organ lessons also gave me great joy. Dr. Schmidt, in connection with many interested English and American officials, got permission to start preparing for the first great musical performance after the war, the *Messiah*. Being a student of Director Schmidt, I was automatically in the Bach and oratorio choir. Since more singers were needed, I could invite my sister Edith and friend Friedel to join the oratorio choir.

Every Monday night we rehearsed under this gifted conductor. Never had I heard these heaven-like choruses and music. As more than 100 voices blended together in clear, pure harmony, lifting their hearts in praise and adoration, I was overwhelmed by the Spirit-filled, powerful words and music. One rehearsal night, singing, "Surely, surely, He bore our sins and suffered our pain," I couldn't sing anymore. Tears streamed down my face. I remembered my mama saying after we had heard *Saint Matthew's Passion* in Danzig, "Maybe after the war is over, you will hear the most beautiful oratorio, the *Messiah* by George Handel." Here I was myself singing in the choir, but where were my mother and father? In heaven? Would they know anything about this?

I could not regain my composure and left the

rehearsal, letting my tears flow freely until once more I found peace and strength. It was enough that the Lord of lords knew it all. I left my loved ones in His loving, merciful hands.

———————

The days grew shorter; fall was here. With food still so scarce, the main foods were potatoes and some other vegetables. We had to stand in line for hours sometimes but could get only what was available at that time. We became inventive. If we could buy some yeast with a little parsley, we cut it up in small pieces, mixed it and called it liver sausage. Cream of wheat cooked with water and a little parsley was called goose lard. These both were substitutes for lunch meat, eaten on our one loaf of bread a week, for which we often stood for hours in line. Sometimes the supply was gone before my turn came.

One day I was told to come early in the morning to get some bread, so I was right there at the bakery at 7 o'clock. When the store was opened, I got my bread and gladly ran home to cut a slice of that fresh, warm bread. I cut through the bread—and found a slimy blue string sticking to the slice of bread, and it stunk.

My stomach turned. I couldn't figure out what had happened to it, whether it was old flour or had worms in it. So much for bread on that day.

One morning I went from our custodian apartment to the big apartment building to wash our laundry. As I walked down the stairs, I heard someone say: "Oh, Pastor Walter, I am so happy to see you."

My heart stopped for a second. Could it be our family's neighbor, Pastor Walter, who had been taken away by the Gestapo? Surely not! I set my laundry down and went up the stairs, following the sound, which came out of one of the apartments on the second floor. I could not contain myself. I knocked at the door. A lady opened it, and I recognized her as the daughter of Pastor Walter.

"My name is Magdalene Krüger from Luisental, in Langfuhr."

Her face lit up. "Fraulein Krüger, what are you doing here? What a joy to see you!"

A dark curtain covering a door frame was pulled to the side, and Pastor Walter stepped out. He was still in hiding from the Nazis who remained free, because of all the information he knew about them. He had been ordered to work in the office of the concentration camp in Dachau. He had "better treatment" than other prisoners because of the cross of bravery he had earned in the First World War. When he and his daughter asked how my parents were, I could only shrug my shoulders. Pastor Walter promised me that they too would pray for my parents.

"They still might be alive. God looks after His own," he said.

My six weeks of group organ lessons were finished, and I, the youngest, together with five other adult students, received my certificate as an assistant organist. Dr. Schmidt encouraged me to go on with my studies and recommended the Church Music School in Hanover which had just opened up. Since I had to be there for classes three days a week, I would stay at the school and be a boarding student on those days. Oh, what an opportunity! I was so excited. With a letter from my professor also suggesting a scholarship, I took the train to Hanover. Would a dream like that come true for me?

As I left the remains of the almost totally bombed-out railroad station, all around me I saw the ruins of houses. One could hardly recognize where the streets had been; there were only pathways around the heaps of rubble. I asked my way around and finally arrived in Kleefeld, a district near a wooded park, where the music school had opened, using the parsonage of a beautiful old church building for the studies.

I was so thirsty to learn and to know more about the great compositions and their authors. I even took some lessons in choir conducting. The organ teacher was a former student of the great composer Max Reger. How fortunate we students were to have lessons with him! I thought sometimes, *All this can't be true*, but I realized that God had His hand in it all. My heart was filled with gratitude.

# CHAPTER 8

# Who Is That Man?

*Behold, the eye of the LORD is upon them that fear him, upon them that hope in his mercy. (Psalm 33:18)*

It was late fall, and the nights were getting cold. Uncle Fritz came to visit us one day and announced that a truck would be coming on the weekend to bring us some cut wood from his war-damaged hunting ground, where many partly burned trees had to be removed.

"Now you will have something to burn during the winter," he said.

The truck came on the following Saturday afternoon, and Edith and I started to unload the black, half-burned wood. I threw it piece by piece down through the open basement window. From there Edith threw the wood into the coal cellar. Our arms and hands were black, and soon the dust darkened our faces as well. We couldn't help laughing as we worked. "Magdchen," Edith yelled, "you look like a chimney sweep."

I laughed. "And you look like his wife," I yelled back.

Suddenly I felt I was being watched. Out of the corner of my eye, there on the sidewalk I saw the figure of a man leaning on his bicycle.

Out of deep-set eyes he stared at us. *Why is he staring at us?* I thought for a second. Then like a bolt of lightning it hit me. It was my father.

"Papa!" I cried as I jumped from the truck and ran down the driveway. Edith climbed out of the window and was right beside me. We flung our arms around our papa. He just clung to us.

As if with one voice we cried, "Where is Mama?"

"She is not here," Papa said with a weak voice, holding onto the handlebar of his bicycle.

"Where is she?" we wanted to know. My knees almost buckled.

"She is alive, though not well. But Oma, Opa and Aunt Lydia are here in Celle at Gertrud's house," he said. "I have to rest awhile, and then you and I have to go over the border and get her. She had to stay in Bad Freienwalde at Uncle Wilhelm's house. Aunt Mariechen stayed with her. Mama's legs were very bad and one had almost turned black. The doctor wanted to amputate the leg, but Mama did not let him. We trust our heavenly Father."

We got our father up the long stairs to our apartment. It took his last bit of strength. He looked like one of the prisoners from the concentration camp.

"Girls," he said, "I have lice."

That was nothing new to us, and we knew how to get rid of them. The main thing was to build up his strength. He couldn't turn his neck around and asked me to look at the back. I saw a huge boil about one inch in diameter, highly infected. He had also smaller ones like the ones we had on our arms from being undernourished. With washings and hot compresses of vinegar and salt we would gradually get the infection down and under control.

Papa described to us how the Russians had destroyed almost the entire city—our beloved Danzig—with the Stalin Organ (a powerful weapon consisting of about forty rockets mounted on a platform. All the rockets were fired at one time, leaving in ruins everything in their path). Afterward they had sheltered thirty-five refugees in our house, mostly women from our Baptist church in Danzig. Often the Russian soldiers came to search for the younger ones, but with two small hidden basements beneath the house, accessible only by lifting up a wooden lid in the floor (kept concealed by a rug), they were quite safe underneath. Our beautiful, high, wrought-iron garden fence with its spear tips was ridden down by their tanks so they could drive in between the homes from one street to another. Our back yard was totally demolished.

"Anything about Fraulein Fischbeck?" I asked.

"The roof of her house was damaged," Papa said. "Opa and I went over there and carried her into our house, and she lay in the little guest room, which you had occupied before you left. As she was totally crippled with arthritis, her heart got worse and her strength ebbed away. The Lord took her home in the springtime. No caskets were available, with thousands of dead all over the city, so we wrapped her in a large white sheet," Papa said. "She has a good and safe place underneath the sweet cherry tree in the garden. She talked often about you. Mama will tell you more."

With tears running down my face I looked at Papa. "How about you? You look like you are eighty years old instead of fifty-nine."

His hair was grey and straggly; he was bitten by lice and covered with boils. Our once-so-strong papa, always perfectly dressed, was now wearing pants tied together over frail, bony hips and the remains of worn-out shoes on his feet. We hugged him again softly, so as not to hurt him.

"Girls," he said, "I have to lie down. I have no more strength left."

Apologizing for not having thought of this earlier, we quickly heated up a pail of water so he could wash up. We wished we could have had a bathtub and hot water in the tap, but these were luxuries at that time.

Exhausted, he fell into the bed and into a deep sleep. Still hardly believing that our papa was with us, we peeked into the room once in a while to see if he was all right. He slept late into the morning. With hearts overflowing with thanksgiving, we finished emptying the truck. Now we had more purpose than ever to see that we were prepared for the winter, and most of all to get our mother from behind Berlin in the East Zone.

The same evening Edith and I walked across town to Gertrud's house and found our sweet little Oma and Opa there, also Aunt Lydia, my mother's youngest half sister. Oh, there was such hugging! The two aunts, my father's sisters, gave up their beds and slept with the children.

"Your father did superhuman things for all of us," Oma said. "Without him none of us would have made it. We got separated one time when he took your mama back to Bad Freienwalde, and I thought that was the end for us. Someone took us into an overfilled refugee camp, but they had no room. Yet the Lord provided for us to stay in a little barrack beside the office. We kept praying for your father and mother but heard nothing of them. Then a few days later, we went over to the food kitchen to get our cup of tea and a piece of bread—and there stood your papa in front of us. He had gone through all the camps searching for us! I never loved the looks of your papa more than in that moment. We all laughed and cried together."

My Aunt Lydia, who had a little mental handicap, added, "Your father always made us walk at night and the night is there to sleep and not to walk."

"Yes," Oma said. "But he borrowed a wheelbarrow or hand wagon—once even a baby buggy—to take us from one village to another and packed me on top of all the luggage. During the day the Russian soldiers tried to rob the people."

Opa had already lain on the bed and was snoring in peace.

We went back to our apartment. Listening at the door we heard a soft snoring there too, but we still had to take one more look at Papa. He was fine, and our hearts were filled with thanksgiving to our heavenly Father for bringing our loved ones safely to us.

The next morning after our father and grandparents came, we notified Uncle Fritz. He quickly came over with his bicycle, bringing a little bit of food with him. Since he was well-known in town, he had some connections we didn't have.

Just two days later Papa said, "Girls, I think we should prepare to get your mother and the others. I feel rested and a bit stronger."

We had eagerly waited for this decision. Papa's two sisters there at Gertrud's house were also now courageous enough to try to go with us over the border and back home to Bad Freienwalde, where our mother was. Papa made his plans to cross over the border where it would be the safest, without being caught by the Russian guards. He had gained experience when they came over to us through the border from East to West Germany. He had met and talked to others on his months-long journey, sometimes helped by a farmer with a horse and wagon, who would pick up my old grandparents while my father and Aunt Lydia walked. They walked most of the 300-kilometer exodus! He also told us that he went to Gommern, near Magdeburg, where he had hoped to find Edith and me.

He had heard the news from Aunt Helene's mother that Uncle Bruno and his family had tried to get away, but without success, and finally had made the desperate decision to end their lives.

Papa asked if there were two girls with them and had been told that there were. "The blonde

was here for several weeks," she told him.
"Then came her sister, who took her to Celle
only a few days before the Russians moved in.
If they had stayed here, maybe all of them still
would be alive. Hannelore wanted so much to
live. But the two girls never came back."

"That gave me new hope," Papa told us later,
"that I would find my daughters. To see you
here, healthy, though with a little black on your
faces, was worth all the trouble. The Lord kept
me going with my last strength. Now we have
to get to your mother."

I hoped that what little I was allowed to share
about my faith in God in my uncle's house may
have changed their hearts about God—maybe at
least Uncle Bruno's and Hannelore's. But only
my heavenly Father could know that.

A poem formed in my heart:

I didn't know this was your way for me.
So you would use me there . . .
I didn't know.
I tried to share You are the One to trust,
For You are love and grace and mercy;
Oh, Lord, You know if they had called on
         You
While in despair.
I prayed they would.
In Your loving plans
You took Your trusting child away from
         there
I knew You would.

# CHAPTER 9

# He Shall Give His Angels . . .

*For he shall give his angels charge over thee,*
*to keep thee in all thy ways. (Psalm 91:11)*

Papa made it very clear to Edith and me that we had to make ourselves look terribly ugly—not pretty *at all*—to go over to the East Zone for my mama. I put some dark blue ointment around one eye, wearing a black patch over it. I hid my hair under a dark kerchief. Together with my two aunts we took the train and arrived at the border town of Helmstedt, only one hour away. Refugees were everywhere, trying to find a guide they could trust, who would lead them through the wooded area around the guard posts.

All kinds of stories came to our ears of fami-

111

lies being separated, girls being taken away and
raped, "guides" who first took pay from the
refugees and then from the guards to lead refugees their way.

A little country school nearby was opened
and set up as an overnight emergency shelter.
It was getting dark, so we found a place there
for my aunts to sit. Desks and seats were all occupied by people huddling together. Edith and
I found a long narrow bench where we could
stretch out a little.

Papa had prayed with us and asked for the
Lord's protection over our journey. He often
instructed us that we should not say a word in
case we should run into the guards. Having
worked for the Russian officers in Danzig, he
was also put in charge of the evacuation of the
last people who stayed in our house. He had
learned a few Russian words in order to com-
municate.

We tried to sleep a little. There was always
soft talking around us. Some people left; some
people came. Finally after midnight, I must
have fallen asleep. But suddenly as clear as a
bell I heard these words: "For he shall give his
angels charge over thee, to keep thee in all thy
ways."

I sat up straight and looked around the dimly
lit room. No one was standing there, but that
voice was so clear.

Softly I called, "Papa."

"Yes," he answered quietly.

"We can go over the border."

"How? Do we have a guide?"

"No," I said. "I just woke up and clearly heard these words: 'He has given His angels charge to keep thee in all thy ways.' I know we can go."

Papa believed his youngest daughter.

While Edith led one aunt and I the other one, carrying their little suitcase, we tried to follow the small path into the woods. Papa's flashlight gave a little light to our steps. It was a damp and foggy November morning, about 5:30. We walked very calmly; I had no fear. Then unexpectedly a bright light was thrown on my dad. I was hiding my face behind my aunt's shoulder when I heard "*Stoi.*"

Papa stopped and we followed suit. We had walked right into the Russian guards, who had stepped out of their booth.

They asked Papa some questions, half German, half Russian. He explained that we wanted to go back to Bad Freienwalde to his wife, our mother. His two sisters also lived there.

They asked for whiskey. Papa had gotten some from my uncle, mixed with water. They motioned him to drink, to make sure it was not poison. He took a sip.

They smiled and took the whiskey—and gave us a sign to pass on by.

*Will they shoot us in the back?* I wondered. We walked along the path, which went downhill.

Just when I thought they could see us no more,
I turned around to look back, and I thought of
Lot's wife, who turned into a pillar of salt. But
the two soldiers just stepped into their guard
booth and we were free to go!

The Lord's angels had led us through!

Oh, how we thanked our dear Lord for being
with us.

Coming out of the woods, we saw something
white sticking out of the dark earth. I picked it
up. It was a piece of a sugar beet! I brushed the
dirt off on my pants and we each had a bite.
Oh, that tasted so good!

Not knowing where we were, we looked
around and saw a little farmhouse. I offered to
ask for directions. An older woman answered
the door.

"Come in, girls," she said. "Soon the soldiers
around the village will look for people in this
area."

My father and aunts also came in, and sure
enough, we saw the soldiers through the window, racing on horses over the fields. Again we
realized our heavenly Father had kept His
promise, and that gave us so much peace.

The little railroad station was just across the
field, and we found that a train to Berlin
would arrive in about an hour. We waited for
the right moment to walk over to the station.
We mingled with the large number of people
who were waiting there. Shortly before the

arrival of the train, Russian soldiers came into that small waiting hall to check us out. We were looking down, holding on to our aunts' arms and were overlooked, but some others had to step out.

Arriving in Berlin, the heart of Germany, the place where Hitler's commands and decisions went into every corner of Germany and beyond, was a very special experience.

All we could see of the city were ruins. We got out in one of the huge halls at the train station, where the roofs had big holes. The train to Bad Freienwalde would come in a few hours. Since mail service had not yet been restored, we used the time between connections to deliver a secret letter. Countess von Kanitz, whom Edith had worked for, had given her the address of the wife of a bishop who had been working in the West with the Christian Ecumenical Council. She still lived in the French sector of Berlin, and her husband had entrusted Edith with a letter for her.

We were informed that the address was close to the train station. As in Hanover there were more rubble and ruins than houses standing, and only little winding pathways led around the rubble to some walls still standing, where one could expect someone to live.

The ringing of the doorbell on a beautiful carved front door gave a hollow echo. Someone opened the door, which had a security chain, allowing us to see only a pair of eyes, and asked, "May I help you?"

Edith carefully said, "I have greetings from Countess Kanitz."

The lady smiled and opened the door wide. We went in and introduced ourselves. Edith pulled the letter out of her coat, and quickly the bishop's wife hid it in her dress.

"Thank you so much. Did anyone watch or follow you?"

"We know of no one," Edith answered.

Stepping outside, we said, so anyone could hear us, "So we have to go around that corner and then straight down the road? Thank you very much."

This was actually the way back to the railroad station. The others were glad to see us back again and soon we were on the way to Bad Freienwalde.

———

It seemed we could not move fast enough to get to my aunt's house, where our mother was. Uncle Wilhelm opened the door. After quickly greeting us, he told us that our mother was in bed upstairs. We softly took two steps at a time and without knocking, quietly opened the door. Never will I forget that sight.

Mama was supported by white cushions, hands folded over her Bible, half sitting in bed, an expression of seeing a vision on her face. Her beautiful dark eyes looked straight at us.

With two steps we were at her bedside and gently embracing our beloved mother. As if in a dream her hands touched our heads and shoulders, and over and over again she whispered, "Oh, my dear Lord, what a joy, what a joy!"

Then we realized others were present: my Aunt Mariechen on the chair in the corner, Tante Malkowski, a friend from our church at home, and her daughter, Ingeborg. They had just been in prayer for Papa and my grandparents, not knowing if they had ever made it to the West or if they had found any one of us alive.

The joy was indescribable. When Papa came upstairs in the room and bent over his wife, Mama just hugged him, saying, "Otto, you are my best."

Brushing off her tears of joy, he answered, "The Lord has been my strength and our guide. Without Him I would not be here—none of us would."

We shared a little of our experiences, and then asked Mama if she would be able to travel.

Her answer was, "The Lord has brought you here and He will bring us also over there. And you are now at my side."

Aunt Mariechen asked if we had anything to eat.

"Nothing but a piece of sugar beet."

"The bakery down the street opens up at 2 p.m. You have to go right away and stand in line. Stand at different places in the line so each of you will get a loaf of bread."

We went and saw that there was already a line along the sidewalk. We took our places. Before us stood a man in an old, worn-out suit. His dark wavy hair hung down to his shoulders and seemed to be alive with lice. They were crawling all over him, even falling off onto the ground.

I had never seen anything like that. He seemed not to care at all. Only once in a while he brushed his hand over his lice-infested beard. I wondered, *Who are you? . . . What has happened in your life that you look so totally unconcerned? Have you not found your loved ones yet . . . or are they all dead?* Compassion filled my heart. "Edith, look," I said softly. She shrugged her shoulders in unbelief.

The man got his bread, not saying a word. People stepped back when he passed the line. When each of us had a loaf, we walked out of the bakery. There, walking slowly, as if carrying a heavy burden, was that man. I could not hold back.

"Sir, you can get help at the Red Cross. They will give you something for the lice. God also will help you. You can call on Him."

There was no life in his sky-blue eyes. His soft, flushed complexion suggested that he might be a young man in his mid-thirties. He looked into my face and, without saying a word, slowly walked on. He was a picture of hopelessness, symbolic of so many who had lost home and loved ones and had been misled by empty promises of a ruthless government. Even worse, he was one of the lost, with no knowledge of Jesus Christ, his only Savior. I would never forget this pitiful picture.

—————

We arrived the next day in Berlin. There were hundreds of people trying to get on a train to the West. Mama, my Aunt Mariechen, Mrs. Malkowski and Ingeborg waited on one of the sidewalks in the terminal, while Edith and I found out that a train would soon leave to Braunschweig.

From talking to people we had heard that the passenger trains were only taking Allies from the American-, English- and French-occupied sectors of Berlin over the border into the West. All others (civilians) had to get off before the border and try on their own to get through, as we had done on the way to the Russian Zone.

Every one of us moved to the other track. Except for one big army sack, my parents had no luggage and my aunt and the others had only a little handbag to call their own. The train moved slowly in, already filled up, yet hundreds more wanted to get on. Edith and Ingeborg pushed Papa, my aunt and her mother into the wagon. They even got the big sack on. Mama was very weak, and I found a little ledge of a luggage-receiving platform where she could sit down.

There she sat, calm and peaceful, her little black purse dangling from her arm, her hands folded. I prayed quietly too: *Lord, You have to find a way for Mama to get on this train, or I'll have to stay behind with her and wait for another train. There are no more trains going today and it's getting late.*

The passenger cars were all filled up with civilians. Some people helped others to climb through the windows. I looked a little to the left and saw a mail official standing in the open door of the mail car.

Slowly I approached him. "Sir, is it possible that my mother could sit on that large box there until we get to the border? She is so weak and has a bad leg and could never get into the overcrowded car."

"I am sorry, but that is forbidden. Only military mail may be transported here," he said.

"But my mother would do nothing wrong in there. Please!" I pleaded.

He looked over to Mama. A train official sounded the whistle.

"Come in," he said with a motion of his hand.

I led her the few steps to the mail car. No one saw this but God.

The train started to move. I ran to the next passenger coach where Edith called, "Magdchen, come here."

Some helpful arms reached out of the window and pulled me in before the train picked up speed. A big load was now off my shoulders.

We arrived near the border in the late afternoon and all the people had to leave the train. We knew from others that an empty coal freight train from Berlin would soon be coming through. People were lining up on both sides of the tracks.

Aunt Mariechen came to me and said, "Here, Magda. I always wanted you to have this gold ring. It has a sapphire stone. If I do not get through, at least you can have that ring."

I could not believe my eyes. Me! Having such a beautiful, valuable piece for myself! "Auntie, I would rather swallow it than ever to allow anyone to take it away from me!" I said, overwhelmed with joy. "But you will make it. Don't say that you will stay behind."

"Well, anyhow, it is yours."

A train appeared in the distance. People moved nervously to make sure they could hop into the empty wagons and hide to get over the border to the West. I put the ring into my mouth.

The train slowed down, waiting for the tracks to be changed. There were some English

soldiers trying to hinder the people from getting on.

"No one can get on," one called. "The border
guard will throw you out and put you into the
camp."

*My English will help,* I thought. "Please, sir,
my mother is so weak and sick. We just got her
here to come and live with us in the West. We
are from the Hanover area."

He looked at me and thought it over, not
able to hinder the others from climbing into the
wagons in the front. He lifted his hand. "I am
not responsible for what will happen to you."

"Thank you," I called.

Suddenly I realized that my ring was missing. "Oh, no!" I cried. "My ring is gone."

We all looked over the gravel stones beside
the track where I had walked while talking to
the soldier at the slow-moving train. After I had
taken it out of my mouth, it could have fallen
out of my hand anywhere. We looked and
looked. No ring.

Aunt Mariechen said, "Well, Magda, better
give up. You had your ring for a short while.
We have to get on the train before it starts moving faster."

I lingered, still searching the ground.

"Come on!" Papa called. "The last boxcar is
approaching!"

Edith and Ingeborg climbed up and pulled
the bolt out of the door. Then they helped Papa

and Mama and the others up. I, still looking, was the last one. Trying to hide my disappointment, I went to huddle with the others in the corner of the black, dusty boxcar.

The freight train picked up a little more speed, but a few minutes later it stopped. No one dared to stand up and look over the wall for fear of being seen by the Russian border guard.

There was absolute silence. Then we heard shouts and screaming. We had been told there was a barbed wire enclosure in the yard for those people who were caught. My heart beat so loudly I thought the guards would hear it. What would happen if they caught us?

Every minute the shouts came closer. We huddled very low, holding our breath and praying silently. I watched a hand reaching over the wall to pull the bolt out of the door. At that moment a whistle blew, and with a strong jerk the train started to move. The hand let go, and with an angry shout the Russian soldier jumped down.

The train gained full speed again. Suddenly from the other side, two tall men jumped over the wall and sat in the other corner, saying nothing. We knew after a few minutes that we were over the border and safe in the West Zone. A gentle rain moistened our coal dust-blackened faces. Mama started to sing: *"Oh, das ich tausend Zungen heatte . . .* Oh, for a Thousand

Tongues to Sing!" With grateful hearts we joined her praise. Overwhelmed by all this, I prayed quietly, *Oh, Lord, forgive me for setting my heart on an earthly thing again. It almost made us miss the train. Thank You for bringing us through anyhow.*

Remorseful tears came and I pulled my handkerchief out of the pocket of my jacket.

Then I felt something hard. "My ring!" I shouted with astonishment and excitment. I must have unconsciously taken it out of my mouth and slipped it into my pocket. Feeling so unworthy of God's love and understanding, I cried softly, *Oh, Lord, thank You for allowing me to have this ring.* I suddenly realized that the Lord had used this incident to get us into the last box car. Then seeing that I was sorry and asking His forgiveness, He let me have the ring again. I had learned my lesson and accepted the ring gratefully out of His merciful hands.

A little later the freight train ended in Braunschweig. We looked over the wall. The passenger train station was far on the other side and many tracks had to be crossed. How would we get Mama and the big sack over to the other side, to the passenger terminal?

The two men who had jumped into our car got out of the corner and opened the bolt with ease. One took the sack on his shoulder and the other carried Mama in both arms. With long, strong steps they passed over the tracks; we could hardly keep up and wondered where they would put our mother.

At the passenger train terminal they set Mama and the sack down—and then they were gone. Bewildered, Mama looked around. "Where are the two men?" she gasped. "I couldn't even thank them. What strong men they were." With wondering eyes, she whispered, "Could they have been angels?"

None of us could see them anywhere. They had simply vanished.

"They must have been God's angels," we echoed with amazement. Though we couldn't understand it, we believed it.

"For he shall give his angels charge over thee, to keep thee in all thy ways" (Psalm 91:11). God always keeps His promises.

A map of medieval Danzig. "Your regiment is of the best nobility, while the supreme power rests with the people."

Krüger house on Luisental #8 in Danzig, Langfuhr

The Krüger family, 1931. In the back are Anneliese, Ruth, Heinz and Karl, and in front are Edith, Otto, Gertrud and Magdalene.

The Krüger family, 1940. Heinz, Anneliese, Gertrud, Ruth, Magdalene, Otto, Edith and Karl This was the last gathering before the war tore the family apart.

The view from *Karls Hoehe* where Magdalene watched the bomb attack on the Westerplatte on September 2, 1939. The Baltic Sea is in the background.

Ursula Rosenthal and Magdalene with their bantam chicken

Stairs to the famous City Hall where school children waited to see Hitler's parade
(also pictured in the November 1939 issue of *National Geographic*,
where Magdalene is second from the left.)

Magdalene's grandparents and a little friend on the balcony of their home

The pipe organ in the *Stadtkirche* in Celle where Handel's *Messiah* was performed after the war.

*Garnison Kirche*, where Magdalene and Gunter were married. It was the home church for many Baptist refugees in Celle.

Cousin Gertrud with her children, Dieter, Siegrid and little Gertrud

Magdalene's godly piano teacher, Fraulein Fischbeck

Heinz Krüger, back from Siberia, with his wife, Marle

Magdalene's helpful relatives, Uncle Fritz and Aunt Else (in the background)

Leben wir, so leben wir dem Herrn,
Sterben wir, so sterben wir dem Herrn.
Darum wir leben oder sterben,
so sind wir dem Herrn.

Wir erhielten die unfaßbare Nachricht, daß unser einziger, unvergeßlicher Sohn, unser lieber Bruder, Enkel und Neffe

Panzerschütze

## Günter Klinksiek

im Alter von 18 Jahren, nach zweitägigem Einsatz im Westen, am 18. Dezember 1944 den Heldentod fand.

Wer aber beharret bis ans Ende, der wird selig.

In tiefer Trauer

**Familie Klinksiek**

zugleich im Namen aller Anverwandten

Bad Oeynhausen, Bülowstr. 2, im Januar 1945.

Die Trauerfeier findet am 4. Februar in der Christuskirche, Horst-Wessel-Str., statt.

Wir erhielten die unfaßbare Nachricht, daß unser lieber, einziger, unvergeßlicher Sohn, unser lb. Bruder, Enkel und Neffe, Panzerschütze

Günter Klinksiek

im Alter von 18 Jahren nach zweitägigem Einsatz im Westen am 18. Dez. 1944 den Heldentod fand. / In tiefer Trauer: Familie Klinksiek zugleich im Namen aller Verwandten.

Bad Oeynhausen, Bülowstr. 2, im Januar 1945.

Trauerf., 4. 2., Christuskirche, Horst-Wessel-Straße.

## Gunter's memorial service program

"For if we live, we live to the Lord,
"and if we die, we die to the Lord,
"Therefore, whether we live or die,
"We are the Lord's."
We received the inconceivable news that our only unforgettable son,
our dear brother, grandson and nephew,
Tank gunner
Gunter Klinksiek
At the age of 18 years, after two days in combat at the West front on
December 18, 1944, found his heroic death.
"But he that endureth to the end shall be saved"
In deep mourning
Family Klinksiek
Also in the name of all relatives
Bad Oeynhausen, Bulowstr. 2, in January 1945
The Memorial Service takes place February 4, in the Christ Church, Horst
Wessel Str.

Gunter and Magdalene's wedding photo, April 30, 1950

Magdalene and Gunter visit Edith and Magdalene's parents at their new customs position at the Dutch border.

Friedel and Magdalene

Katitza, Magdalene's widowed prayer partner, remarries her brother-in-law

Magdalene, Gunter and their first-born, Karl Gunter, summer 1951

The Klinksiek family, around 1952
Margaret, Gunter and Rosie are in the background, Karoline
(Gunter's mother), Erika and Hermann (Gunter's father) are in the foreground.

The Klinksiek Bakery and Confectionary, Bad Oeynhausen, Westfahlen

Gunter, Magdalene and Karl dining on the way to Canada, 1953

Letzter Gruss vor der Abfahrt aus
BREMEN

TSS „NEPTUNIA"

The *TSS Neptunia*, which took the Klinksieks over the ocean

Two Klinksiek men on the
way to Canada

Peter's baby carriage—
ham included!

Welcome to Windsor, Canada! Magdalene (center) with Edith and Anneliese
(left) and Pastor Jack Watts (right), a humble man later to become General
Secretary of the Canadian Fellowship of Baptist Churches.

Edith looking after the Klinksieks' wellbeing, holding Margaret,
our first child born in Canada

The Klinksieks sing in Sunday school. Aunt Annie is in the background.

God's special blessing on 1 acres—
our Cape Cod home on North Talbot Road

Gertrud and Otto Krüger's 50th wedding anniversary photo, around 1966

The Klinksieks around 1979—
Peter, Margaret, Madgalene, Gunter, Susan and Karl

Lou Sutera, Magdalene, Gunter and Ralph Sutera

Magdalene and Gunter's home in Ontario
"God takes care of the landscaping, changing its dress to the most
beautiful colors of the season."

# CHAPTER 10

# God Is
# Everywhere

*And seek not ye what ye shall eat, or what ye
shall drink. . . . Your Father knoweth that ye
have need of these things. (Luke 12:29-30)*

Without any further difficulties we got to
the next train, which would take us to
Celle. And with a borrowed hand wagon we
got Mama and the big army bag safely home to
our apartment. Among the pillows were some
bed linens, towels, tablecloths and a few pieces
of cutlery. But then I spotted something very
familiar to me—the little tablecloth I had embroidered for Mama's birthday when I was just
ten years old.

Mama said, "Sometimes my heart was heavy,
though I had trusted you into the Lord's

hand—that's when I pressed this work of love from your little hands to my heart and felt close to you."

She continued, "Magda, sit down. This is the last gift from Fraulein Fischbeck to you. Just before she died she said, 'Give this to my darling little Magdalene with all my love.' "

It was a narrow gold brooch with a beautiful green turquoise stone in the middle. I had left all my clothes with all my jewelry in Gommern, believing we would be back in two days. This lovely brooch was such a beautiful memory from my beloved piano teacher, who had always prayed over my hands.

Mama and Papa were very weak. Hardly any food was available. The best thing for them was to rest.

Though the Christmas season drew near, we had nothing to prepare. There was nothing in the stores; they all were still closed. But we had prepared hearts for the greatest gift God gave to mankind, our precious Savior, Jesus Christ. Though we had lost our beautiful home and homeland and everything we loved and called our own, we had never lost the presence of our Lord, and in His loving mercy and grace He had led us together again.

What a great joy it was also that a former German prisoner, also from Danzig, who had been released from Siberia came to see my parents and told them that my oldest brother Heinz was still alive. Our trustful prayers were rewarded again! God had kept my brother alive amidst thousands who did not survive the cold winters and torturous treatment.

It seemed that God wanted to put my broken family together again. A few mornings later I looked out the window and saw a woman slowly walking toward our front door. It looked as if she were carrying a heavy burden on her shoulders, hardly able to take another step. I suddenly recognized my sister Ruth!

I raced down the stairs to embrace her. Difficult and hard times as a Red Cross nurse had left signs of strain and tiredness on her face. As she shared just a little of what had happened, my heart went out to her. Only God's grace had carried her until this day.

At least we were all alive, and the Lord in His faithfulness would further lead each of us, including our brother Heinz, along His way as we trusted him. And one day when we see Him face to face, our brother Karl will be there too.

In order to take care of my parents I had to discontinue my studies in the Church Music School in Hanover. But I could still stay in the Bach oratorio choir.

The last rehearsal for the *Messiah* came and with it the Philharmonic Orchestra from Hamburg and some of the well-known soloists.

One of them was Elizabeth SchwartzKopf, a distant relative of Countess Kanitz. The next evening the *Stadtkirche*, "our cathedral," was filled from the high balcony to the last standing place in the back. For the first time, seven months after the end of the war, we saw the occupying military, the victors of this destructive war, sitting peacefully among the losers, the civilians. Truly a strange atmosphere prevailed— a mixture of fear, skepticism, hidden anger and shame—yet a sense of joy could not be denied. Dr. Schmidt entered, and the uneasy audience grew silent.

The orchestra's overwhelming introduction started and melodic harmonies flooded over all who had one desire—to hear the message of the *Messiah*, the Christ-child born for the whole world, the Redeemer who died for all.

As the sound of the "Hallelujah Chorus" rose majestically to the highest ceiling, suddenly the soldiers stood up. For a moment fearful surprise crossed the faces of the civilians. Then some civilians joined the military until everyone stood in awe and adoration before the King of kings, Jesus Christ our Lord.

My voice was choked. Dr. Schmidt obviously knew what was going on behind him. Tears were streaming down his face while he brought the choir to its glorious end. "For the Lord God Omnipotent reigneth forever and ever! Hallelujah! Hallelujah!"

Mama and Papa had not been able to attend this beautiful Christmas presentation but were so grateful that Edith and I were privileged to be a part of the overwhelming experience.

Uncle Fritz brought us a little Christmas tree. We tried to get some real candles but found none. We had talked sometimes to three young Hungarian soldiers who had been with the occupying forces in West Germany and who had passed by our home.

Mama said, "These poor boys. Ask them if they want to sit with us on Christmas Eve. At least we can sing and have a cup of peppermint tea together."

They could understand a little German, so we communicated this idea to them and they accepted. When they saw our empty little tree and that we had no candles, one went back to their quarters and came back with a pack of cigarettes and thin wire. Smiling broadly they tied the white cigarettes to the branches, standing them up like candles. Then out of their pockets they pulled cans of sardines, oranges, a big round loaf of bread and tea bags. We couldn't believe our eyes. We hadn't seen such things for a long time, since our diet was mostly potatoes and vegetables, sometimes milk and—very seldom—a little meat.

They sang Hungarian Christmas songs and we German ones. Papa read the Christmas story, and together we enjoyed the food they had brought—a true surprise of God's love for all of us.

We could tell that they were homesick, especially the youngest one, a nineteen-year-old, who had tears in his eyes. They often came to visit us later on, sometimes even bringing an accordion and some food, which was welcome and much appreciated.

———————

One Saturday Mama said, "Magda, maybe you could go to the butcher and ask for some bones for soup for Sunday."

I stood in line for whatever was available. Before my turn came, it was all gone. I waited till the store was empty, then turned to the woman behind the counter and asked if she could look again, just for a few soup bones. "My parents are so weak," I pleaded. "We would so much love some bones to make a soup for Sunday."

Without a word she turned around, reached underneath the counter, wrapped something into newspaper and gave it to me.

Joyfully unwrapping it in the kitchen at home, I hardly believed what I saw—part of a cow's jaw bone with teeth still in it and one eye staring at me.

I got an idea.

"Mama, Mama, I have hurt my eye," I cried, covering one eye with one hand and holding the eye of the cow in the other.

Mama stared at me and gasped in shock.

I quickly took my hand off my eye so she could see I was all right, but I felt very bad for scaring her with such a bad joke, which could have given my mother a real heart problem.

She forgave me as she always did, but with a little scolding in her voice she said, "You still act like an eighteen-year-old." Then with a little smile on her face she continued, "Just wash the jaw bone well. With onions, carrots, celery and some potatoes, it will make a good soup." We could thank God if this was His choice for our Sunday dinner. It was a delicious soup, though no one else knew what was in it.

---

It was a mild winter in middle Germany, nothing like what we had experienced the year before on my flight during the last weeks of the war. One day when Pastor Brother Kretch, also a refugee, visited us, he announced the good news that a branch of the Evangelical State Church had offered their facilities for our worship services. As he asked my father for advice on this matter, he also wondered if he could get a quartet together.

Papa said, "Oh, yes, with Magda singing soprano, Edith alto and you tenor, I'll sing bass."

Our first song, sung a cappella, was, "The Lord Is My Faithful Shepherd," and we sang it from the depths of our heart. Pastor Kretch also asked Edith and me to come and visit him on the following day to meet his family, who had just arrived from the East Zone.

There he gave us a box called a "CARE" package, which was sent from faithful, loving Christians in America. We hadn't seen anything like that for ages. There were some cans with corned beef, Crisco, milk powder, cocoa, even coffee and a canned ham. Also some clothes were sent to share among refugee believers. We didn't know whom we could thank for these things we needed so desperately. We praised and thanked our Lord and asked Him to bless those over the ocean who did so much good to their brothers and sisters here.

I was so thankful to have a warm winter coat and a Sunday dress, a skirt and a sweater. We profited many times in the coming year from these *liebes packete,* love packages.

My friend Friedel had often come to our meetings. She brought laughter back into my life. Maybe it was because she was just seventeen, but she raised my spirits with her unique ideas and intelligent humor. I liked her suggestion that we make Easter dresses out of white parachute silk and blue-gray striped material, leftovers from the lost war, brought to us by the three Hungarian boys. Under Mama's supervision, we sewed by hand a skirt and blouse and were quite proud of our achievement.

"Have you ever seen the Easter Lamb in the rising sun on Easter morning?" Friedel asked me.

"No, never," I replied.

"I will show you," she assured me.

In the early dawn we went down to the Aller River. There was frost on the grass. In my light blouse I was ice cold, yet the beauty of the rising sun seemed to warm me. Arm in arm Friedel and I looked at the flickering shine of that gigantic fireball rising over the meadow.

"See the Easter Lamb?"

"I can imagine that these jumping sunbeams could be taken for that," I agreed.

We both thought of the women who went early to the grave of our Lord and found it empty.

"Christ is risen!" I said.

"He is risen indeed!" she answered with the customary greeting.

We had to turn our eyes from the high rising sun. Yet the Son of God stayed alive in our hearts. Friedel again coaxed me to follow her in another "good idea."

"They say if you wash your face in flowing water right after the sunrise, you get beautiful skin." And down she bent, splashing the water with her hand onto her face. "Oh, that feels so good," she said.

I followed her trustingly. The water was icy. Still, I washed my face to please her.

When I came home my mother said, "What happened to you? Your face is covered with big red splotches!"

I told her what we had done.

"You two!" she said. "Better come and have something warm to drink. Your skin cannot take a treatment like this one on such a frosty morning."

This was not the last "good idea" that Friedel suggested, but I became more cautious in following her advice.

---

That spring of 1946 business mail service had started, and Papa reported his entry to the Headquarters of Customs Services in West Germany. Soon he was asked for further papers and qualifications from Danzig. After it was proved that he had never joined the Nazi Party, he was offered a job organizing and opening up some customs stations at the German-Dutch border as soon as he was healthy.

We were excited. God rewarded the faithful, steadfast obedience of His servant to his heavenly King. It was not easy to start with nothing. There was no furniture. Everything had been removed during the war or had been partly destroyed. Yet the Lord gave much wisdom to my father, and we girls had to help out to set up the household from scratch. We had straw mattresses (common at that time) and a little wood stove, which was all we had for cooking and for heating the living quarters. Most of the time there was no electricity. It took weeks or months until a telephone could be installed. Yet as soon as Mama was able to leave, she went joyfully to be at her husband's side.

Papa was able to cut hard peat moss for heating their house and for cooking, cutting it from the land beside the customs station where they lived. Though everything was quite primitive, one could feel right at home. As always the day started with a time of meditation and singing, and God blessed His children, giving them much grace and wisdom.

After the first customs station was organized, Papa was transferred to start several more. The administration was very pleased, and after establishing the last of the largest of these offices, he got the highest promotion possible, which entitled him to receive a good pension later on.

Since Mama and Papa had moved, I was the next one to look after my grandparents, who were now in their early eighties. We moved into the apartment of a single lady at the outskirts of Celle. There were four rooms, a kitchen and a bathroom. Each room was occupied by a different party. Our apartment was on the third floor. Oma, who had a hard time climbing the stairs, was glad that I could take care of all the errands.

Since there was no available fuel for the furnace, each room had to have a little wood stove with the chimney put through the window. I had a nice large room for myself, overlooking the highway, containing a couch and a round table with two chairs from my Uncle Fritz. Most important, I had rented a piano for twenty-five marks a month. What a treasure! I could resume my piano studies with a concert pianist in Celle.

Some people started a business out of their home, and I got my first job selling all kinds of buttons to friends and acquaintances. However, I didn't know enough people really to make much money.

The economy was still down and inflation extremely high. No stores were opened; only the black market around the park at the castle was booming. Through the employment office, which had just opened up, I heard about a different job—silk painting on parachute silk. The job was given out for home employment. Since I was pretty good in art, I applied for it and got the job. It was very suitable for me. I could pack 300 to 500 little silk doilies, handkerchiefs, ties and bows—and with them my paints—into a suitcase and paint wherever I was, as long as I brought my assigned quota back at a specified time. I felt really rich that I could take my first earnings and the cigarette stamps from my ration cards and go to the black market and buy my own little alarm clock.

Our church was growing and growing. We had formed a youth group and immediately started to minister to the many young people hanging around in railway stations and on street corners. They searched the endless lists of unregistered refugees for loved ones and friends. Having gone through this trauma ourselves, we could identify and point them to Jesus, who had been our Strength, our Friend and only Hope in all the situations we had gone through.

# CHAPTER 11

# The Desires of My Heart

*Delight thyself also in the LORD, and he shall give thee the desires of thine heart. (Psalm 37:4)*

A young woman, just a little over twenty, had come to our church. Katitza Bojidge from Croatia had been an orphan for most of her youth and now was a new widow.

We immediately took to each other, and she became my best friend. Oh, what a mature Christian she had become! She had lost her German husband shortly after they had fled their country, and she had learned to rely totally on God. Together we saw so many answers to our prayers. She was a seamstress for a fur store whose employees worked out of their homes.

They needed another person to sew, so I got the job. She offered to train me, and together we experienced the toughness of the colt and cow leathers used for the first coats that we sewed for private orders. She told me about the coat designer, an atheist who mocked her when she prayed over her lunch. We thought that together it would be much easier for us to witness to him. Since this man, Herman, was much interested in classical music, I soon had an opportunity to share a little about my faith.

Still, often while bringing me home from work, he tried to make his opposition clear to me. He was interested in the science of astronomy. Whenever he talked, I prayed silently for the right answer so I could share Christ's reality in my life. He was a former lieutenant in the navy and very well educated, so I enjoyed our talks. Since he was a very polite young man, we developed a good friendship, though he was six years older than I.

With electricity still rationed to civilians for the after-midnight hours, we had only candle-light to work by. Herman came to visit me often in the evening, reading poetry, Shakespeare's plays and other literature to me while I continued to work on my silk paintings. He also loved to listen as I practiced at the piano.

I had agreed to let him call me by my first name instead of Miss Krüger, but I kept a clear distance. Oh, how I would have liked it if he would come to know Him whom I loved with all my heart!

One clear winter evening Herman brought me home from work. Knowing a little bit about the stars, I pointed out the Big Dipper, Orion and other beautiful constellations. He added more from his knowledge of astronomy. My heart was so filled with awe and wonder of God's great universe that I couldn't hold back any longer.

"Herman," I said, "you tell me that all these creations came into being on their own. You say you cannot believe in one Creator who would be able to create the manifold wonders of this world. But to me, God is in everything that I see, hear and feel. Think of the great scientists, the greatest composers, writers, the greatest artists being multiplied a billion times and more. This, to me, is a fraction of what God is . . . all-knowing, all-present, all-powerful."

He didn't answer and kept silent till we reached my front door. With a low "Thank you" and a hand kiss, he turned to go home. With inner peace in my heart I felt that God had given me these words to say to him.

My room was cold most of the time since coal was rarely available, and even when it was, it was only for people over seventy. I was glad that my grandma had put a hot water bottle under my blanket. I fell asleep, but I woke up later from a noise like a cracking bang right in my room. Then it was quiet again. With no electricity in the cold room, I didn't want to get up to investigate with candlelight, so I cuddled up deeper under my blanket.

Morning dawned and I crawled out of my bed. My feet touched something icy cold. My beautiful, natural plank floor was covered with ice. I couldn't figure out what had happened! But as it got lighter in the room I saw water dripping from the large water heater under the picture window. The bitter-cold night temperature had entered our apartment building and burst the water pipes, which had not been used since the end of the war. Laughingly I told my grandparents that I now had my own ice palace—I only needed some skates. How grateful I was that I could eat my meals in the warm room where my grandparents lived.

Opa made a fire in my little potbellied stove to thaw the ice out so I could clean up the water before it soaked through to the apartment on the second floor. I couldn't wait until spring finally came and Oma started to plant flowers on the south-side balcony, which our landlady allowed us to share.

───※───

Our youth groups from the Baptist churches had received permission to have the very first large Youth Bible Camp after the war in July 1947, and I was very excited. This would be an opportunity to invite Herman to hear some of the great young preachers. Maybe then he would become a Christian! My sister Edith also got twelve days of holiday from work, and together with most people from our youth group, we went by train to Mellendorf, on the Loens Lake near Hanover, about a one-hour train ride away from Celle. Herman had agreed to visit us on the weekend, since it was also to be my birthday. He blended in quite well with the fellows in our group.

We saw each other during the morning meditation and at meal times. For my birthday he had made me a little mink collar and also bought a large flowerpot, which we placed in the dining room. Though I didn't like to be singled out, I appreciated his courtesy. I hoped that in the time between Friday and Monday, with great men like E.D. Brandt, John Goetze and P. Klempel ministering and counseling, he would be able to make a decision about Christ.

Monday came and Herman had to leave. I walked with him to the little train station.

"Do you understand now what I believe?" I asked eagerly. "Did you have a chance to talk to any of the leaders?"

"Yes," he said. "It was all good, but I still have so many questions. There is so much I don't understand."

"Why don't you just ask Jesus Christ into your life?" I pressed on. "Why don't we pray right here before we reach the train station in the village?"

There was silence.

"Would you pray after me?" I persisted.

"I'm sorry, but I cannot pray."

We reached the end of the woods and the little station. "I hope you still have a good time," he said. "See you in Celle."

I was numb inside.

After coming back to the camp I went to see Carola Geiger, our youth conference counselor. I had told her before of Herman and my great hope for him, and now shared with her my disappointment. She said wisely, "Magdalene, you have to leave this in God's hands and in His timing."

---

It was my turn the next day to help in the kitchen and to serve at the supper table. Coming to a table where several young men were sitting, I tried to hand the plates of soup to them quickly. But there was this handsome fellow with dark hair, who looked straight at me, and then as if he was scared I would spill the plate, he bent to the side. Getting very nervous I blushed—which didn't help—and sure enough, my shaking hand spilled the soup over his knees.

I could have died! Everyone laughed. *How clumsy!* I thought. *I will never serve them again.*

That evening Edith and I were at the girls' quarters loosening up our straw sleeping mattresses when I heard someone playing the accordion. "Listen," I called, trying to hear above the rustling noise. "Who here has an accordion?"

Some girls ran downstairs where there was already a group gathering around a picnic table. I stretched my neck to see who was playing.

*Oh, no! Not this guy again!* I thought.

The playing stopped as he spotted me. "Hey, come here. You can play," he shouted.

And his friend coaxed, "Yes, I heard you play at the youth retreat in Braunschweig."

What I didn't know was that this friend had told him I was a musician and had made a bet with him that he could never get my attention. To prove this untrue, he had borrowed an accordion from one of his friends.

Blushing again, I wanted to withdraw, but the girls pulled me forward and begged me to play, asking for one song after another. I played and we sang till the dusk fell and we had to go to our quarters. After our next morning meditation time, having an hour free, this dark-haired fellow and his friend approached Edith and me.

"I have the accordion again. Can you come and play for us?"

*He must like Edith,* I thought, *and uses the accordion to get to her.*

I played and we sang. I thought he had a beautiful bass voice. Casually he pulled out his wallet and showed me a little news clipping, an obituary from 1945. I read:

> We received the inconceivable news
> that our only unforgettable son,
> our dear brother, grandson and nephew,
> Tank gunner
>
> Gunter Klinksiek
>
> at the young age of eighteen years
> after two days in combat at the West front
> on December 18, 1944, found his heroic death.
>
> In deep mourning,
> Family Klinksiek
> Also in the name of all relatives,
> Bad Oeynhausen Bulow Str. 2
> January 1945
> Memorial Service, February 2 at the
> Christus Kirche (Christ's Church)
> Horst Wessel Str.

"Who is this?" I asked. "Your friend?"
He shook his head.
"Your brother?"
He shook it again. "It's me."

I was puzzled. "You! Is this your name—Gunter Klinksiek?"

"Yes," he said.

"But you are here," I murmured.

"Yes, I was declared dead, but God let me live."

*This is unreal,* I thought, as we had to leave to attend our separate sessions.

The last evening came, and all of us young people gathered in a half circle around a huge bonfire at the edge of the forest overlooking the meadow. It was a beautiful setting—a light evening fog was moving in and the moon coming up made us wish we could stay on even longer. As usual we sang one song after another, and then our leaders asked for testimonies. Many shared the blessings and strength they had received in these days after having experienced the trauma of broken dreams and much hardship in the last two years following the war. Again and again, they expressed their gratitude for God's faithful leading.

Gunter was one who gave a short testimony, mentioning how thankful he was to be here and alive. At the last song we all got up and sang, "Blessed Be the Tie That Binds." All joined hands, and a strong, large hand grabbed mine. I looked down into the flames of the fire and then noticed the feet of someone familiar standing beside me. *Oh, no, not him again,* I thought.

As soon as the song had ended, I tried to locate Edith, but someone called, "Can you wait a moment?"

It was Gunter. "May I have your address?" he asked.

"Why?" I said. "Don't you remember that I had a boyfriend visiting here?"

"No," he said.

"You mean you didn't see him? Everybody knew about it and the big flowerpot he brought, which was in the dining hall."

"No," he said again. "Is he a Christian?"

"Not yet," I replied. "That's why I brought him here."

"How do you know that he is going to be one?" He told me about his friend's unsaved wife, who had taken off with another man while he was in the army. "I watched you," he continued, "and I think we are supposed to become partners for life."

I couldn't believe my ears. "How can you say something like that?" I protested. "I don't even know you!"

"But I think you are meant for me," he insisted.

"Well," I said reluctantly. "We can pray about it." I was trying to put it off, hoping to get out of this and wanting to leave.

"Let's pray right now," he said.

And he put his arms around me. I could not back up since there was a tree behind me. Then he prayed something like, "Thank You, Lord, that You have shown me the right girl for my life."

While he prayed, a strange picture came into my mind. I remembered sitting on our balcony with a pail of salt water, soaking my feet, which had been so sore from the long walk home from work in shoes which did not fit. And I was weary from trying to argue with Herman about my faith. I had prayed, *Oh, Lord, can't You let me meet a Christian man who also loves You like I do?* Thinking of this, a little voice inside said, *Why do you want to resist now? This is a man who is a Christian. You have asked for this.*

And so I prayed aloud, "Lord, I really don't know this man, but if You want us together, You have to put Your love for him into my heart."

With this we parted, and the next morning I gave him my address.

CHAPTER 12

# *Two-Part Harmony*

*Commit thy way unto the LORD; trust also in him; and he shall bring it to pass. (Psalm 37:5)*

On the train ride home my head was spinning. *What am I going to do? What am I going to say to Herman?*

When I got home, Oma opened the door and said, "Mr. Lange has already been here asking for you. He will come back in about an hour."

"Oh," I moaned, "you don't know what happened to me! I met someone at the Bible camp who thinks that God wants us together. We prayed about it, and it seems that's what it's going to be!"

"Oh, my," she said with astonishment.

153

"Oma, when Herman comes again, tell him I am not feeling well," I said.

I went into my room and lay down on my sofa, trying to get my thoughts together. *Oh, Lord, give me wisdom and strength. I do not want to hurt this man; he is so kind. Yet You are my everything. I don't know what my future brings. You know it.*

I became more peaceful inside. Then the doorbell rang again, and I heard Oma open the door and say, "Mr. Lange, my granddaughter is not feeling very well."

Hardly believing it was me, I called, "Oma, that's all right. I feel a little better. He can come in."

And there he stood—with a big bouquet of flowers.

Carefully explaining that I feared our friendship could turn into something deeper, I told him I had asked God to show me what He wanted for me. Then I told him that, totally unexpectedly, God seemed to have brought a man into my life who shared my faith (which Herman knew meant everything to me).

Thanking me for my honesty and the friendship we had shared, he left. I felt like crying. I had cherished our friendship so much and wished that it still could go on. Yet I hung onto the conviction that God knew what was best for me, since He had answered my prayer. *Oh, Lord,* I prayed, *You have Your ways and time. You can still let him remember all that we had talked about You and what he had heard there on the weekend. You can open his heart and take the blindness away.* With that I found peace in my heart.

I told my dear Oma more of the whole situation. Though she was in her eighties, her heart was very young. When someone asked, "Mrs. Liedtke, how old are you?" she would say, "Just eighteen. My heart is always young." She had shared her love story with me. Being left a widow at twenty with two children, she had then married her brother-in-law, who had been widowed twice. Her life was full of excitement.

She had brought up his three boys plus three children from her second marriage but had kept a beautiful sense of humor. Her strong faith in God carried her through many trials and testings. Every morning and evening she and Opa had their meditation time, singing a praise hymn to the Lord before they read the Scripture. Then they always went on their knees to intercede for the lost and for the church's needs. And I often joined them, feeling so secure in their company. My faith also grew stronger because of this.

---

Gunter had said that he would come the next Sunday. Around 2 o'clock the noise of a motorcycle got my attention. Off stepped a tall man in a leather outfit.

*Really, what kind of man is he?* I thought. My heart was beating fast. Carrying a white cake container, he came up the stairs. With a smile he opened the container. I hadn't seen a butter-cream torte since the beginning of the war. What a treat for all of us! Oma thought he was a very handsome, fine young man—and so did I. He told me that his parents had invited me to meet them two weeks later.

When that day came, I took a train to Bad Oeynhausen, about 140 kilometers away from Celle. Gunter was waiting for me in a white suit. *He must work at the hospital. Maybe he is an intern*, I thought.

We drove around the town, which had been occupied by the English Army and was the headquarters of the English sector of Germany. A barbed-wire fence closed off many streets. He showed me his church, the Christus Kirche, just outside the wall of barbed wire, and this fence came within 200 feet of their house, where Gunter stopped the car.

"Come," he said and walked with me to the back door.

To my surprise we stood in a bakery with a big baking oven in front of me and the machinery and cake racks round the wall.

"Do you have to pick up something?" I asked.

"No, this is our bakery, my workplace," he answered.

That explained the white suit.

It was the end of September when I went to see my parents, who were still living at the Dutch border. I wanted to help Mama, whose legs had acted up again and who needed rest. I had written my parents about meeting Gunter, and they agreed that he should come on the following weekend.

I walked the two kilometers to the train station to meet him. I couldn't believe the weight of the wooden suitcase he brought.

"What do you have in there, rocks?"

He only smiled.

My parents liked Gunter right away. He was eager to open his suitcase. Mama's eyes got bigger and bigger as he lifted out of the suitcase a thirty-pound sack of flour, a large piece of ham, bacon and a large smoked sausage—things one could only dream of at that time.

"Oh, the Lord is so good," she said over and over again. "Gunter, are you sure you want to leave all this here?"

He laughed, "My mother feeds pigs from the leftovers of our bakery. That's where the ham and the sausage come from."

Gunter had also brought me a beautiful silver bracelet, handmade from old silver coins, which I cherished very much. In the evening Gunter and I went to a farmer who let my parents have some milk once in a while. Walking across a large field of stubble, we enjoyed the beautiful sunset. I had noticed how much Gunter loved God's creation, just as I did. We sang some songs we knew in two-part harmony. My heart was filled with joy and thanksgiving, and I realized that love for this man had started to grow in my heart.

Coming back home I set the milk on the table and noticed that my silver bracelet was gone. I was shocked. Where could it be? The last time I looked at it was when we crossed the large stubble field to the farm.

"Oh," I moaned, "what should I do?"

Gunter comforted me. "We will go right after sunrise and look for it."

I thought, *There's no chance I'll find it!* But in bed I prayed, *Lord, You know where it is. Do You allow me to have this? I do not want to set my heart on it but it is a gift from the man You sent into my life.*

We got up at sunrise, and when we came to the field we both stood still and prayed that the Lord would lead us even in this vast stubble field to find the bracelet. We had walked maybe a third of it, and there on the dewy, silvery, sparkling ground in front of me was the bracelet! Oh, how we thanked our gracious Father! It seemed like a sign of approval that He restored it to me.

When we came home, we went to Mama's bed, and she rejoiced with us. Sitting down, we sang one of the songs we had sung at Youth Bible Camp in two-part harmony: "Lord our God,

You are our strength, the help in which we are trusting."

Mama listened with tears in her eyes. After we finished she said, "Children, your voices blend together very well. May the Lord use you to His praise."

That evening when Papa went to the sheep stall to feed the sheep, Gunter followed him. When they returned, Papa said with a mischievous smile, "I never thought that someone would ask me for the hand of my daughter in the sheep stall, but you have our blessings. The most important thing is that you both love the Lord."

After Gunter left Monday morning, Mama called me to her bedside and said, "Magda, Gunter is a fine man. He loves his Lord and you. But do not expect an easy life in the bakery business. With your delicate hands and wrists the work might be very hard for you. But I know that the Lord will be at your side."

---

We were engaged on January 25, 1948, the very same day I had become a refugee three years earlier. One could not buy a ring for only money; one had to have a special connection. But Gunter's mother found the solution: "A ham will do it." With the new value of the German mark we got our plain engagement ring, and this gold band would serve also as a wedding ring. How faithful God had been to me with the friends He had given me—and most of all, as I had asked Him, the man who was also a child of God, and whom I now loved dearly.

Three months after our engagement I received a letter from Herman Lange, congratulating us. He thanked me and added that, moved by my steadfast faith and testimony and all that he had heard and seen on that weekend in the Bible camp, he had found Jesus Christ.

He wrote, "All my arguing had to come to an end. No one can get around Jesus Christ. His example and His Spirit alone enfolds the redemption of all mankind. Oh, that all would come to know Him! I am so grateful that I could see the work of God's Spirit in you and in the others. I trust that through the ministry of His Spirit, God's Word will continually guide and teach me."

My heart was so full of thanksgiving that the Lord had answered my prayers to open Herman's heart. Why had this not happened when I first expected it? Only God knew, for He had different plans for my life and for Herman's, who wanted to go back into the East Zone to Dresden to support his sister and widowed mother.

I had started to take Edith's place as nanny in

the house of Count von Kanitz, looking after the six countesses. I marveled when I saw the humble faith of the countess, overseeing a household of ten people including me. The six girls, ranging in age from five to eleven years old, including a set of twins, all had long pigtails, and washing and combing their hair was a real job.

There was much to mend, and every Monday morning at 5 o'clock we started washing laundry by hand—the countess, Fraulein Gertrud (the cook) and myself. One day Frau Graefin (a German name for countess), as the countess asked me to call her, sent me up to the attic. "Fraulein Magda, would you fetch me a bowl of flour? We have a birthday coming up. Fraulein Gertrud will bake a cake." She also gave me a sieve. "Please make sure that you sift the flour into the bowl, then put what is left in the sieve in this bag and bring it down to burn."

A little puzzled, I went upstairs and started to sift one cup after another through the sieve until the bowl was full. But I couldn't believe my eyes when I saw little gray bugs crawling on the bottom of the sieve. I quickly emptied it into the paper bag. After I mentioned this incident in a letter to Gunter, he enclosed in his next letter food stamps for several loaves of bread and flour for the Kanitz family. When I gave this to her, she looked bewildered.

"Where did your fiancé get these?"

I laughed, "Not from the black market. His parents have a bakery and are able to help others."

"Oh," she said, "how faithful is our Lord! Give your fiancé our deepest gratitude."

———————

I tried to collect something for my dowry, but it seemed to be hopeless. Papa had made only a few little connections with some factories at the border which started to weave and had opened a little outlet, so I got some material to sew some bedding.

On my day off I walked to Friedel's apartment and saw a long line of people at the store across the street. The broken windows were boarded with plywood.

I asked somebody, "What's for sale?"

"Apparently they sell towels or some sewing materials."

So I took my place. The line moved slowly. When I got to the door there was a dim light in the back. Moving closer I saw two women and a man behind the counter, and to my greatest astonishment I recognized Mrs. Wolf and her daughter and son, our former neighbors from Luisental #3, across from our house in Danzig.

"Fraulein Krüger!" she called out. Coming around the counter they hugged and kissed me. "We will never forget what your parents did for our father, though it was of no avail. What can we do for you?"

I mentioned that I planned to get married and was trying to buy something for my future household.

"Wait," she said, and a little later I had a big bundle of towels with a barley pattern under my arm.

God seemed to open up more doors to provide for my needs.

A niece of Frau Graefin had moved to Celle and came to live with them, also helping with the children. My job there was now finished, but another opened up.

I worked first in an upholstery business that started to make travel bags. I learned quickly to sew these bags and was able to make myself two large ones for traveling. Then a knitting business opened on the same street, and since the hard material of the upholstery was often causing pain in my fingers, I applied for the job and got it. On a Swiss Passap knitting machine, I knitted my first birthday and Christmas gifts for Gunter. I also knitted for myself some pullovers and cardigans, since I was privileged as an employee to purchase some wool for my own use.

Our church of mostly refugees continued to

grow. We often had more than 300 people in attendance, and a good choir had started. I was asked to be the organist for the services and choir. Though I would have loved to play on a large pipe organ as I had learned, I was grateful to play on this little pedal organ, similar to the one at home, which had been demolished by a grenade. I still enjoyed very much being a member of the Bach choir and taking part in all performances, but our church choir decided to practice on the same night as the Bach choir, and I had to make a decision. My heart was in both places, yet I knew that I had to be where God would like me to serve, in our Baptist church. The peace in my heart confirmed to me that this was God's will. The Lord seemed to reward my decision, giving me opportunity to study piano again.

Some English and Canadian soldiers attended our church services, and one, hearing that I copied classical music off by hand since no music manuscripts were available to buy at that time, ordered some Bach preludes and fugues, some volumes of Schubert and Chopin and other composers for piano. Recommended by Dr. Schmidt, I continued some more studies with a good pianist. Oh, how happy I was!

My dear friend Friedel, who had often attended our church but remained a traditional (but unsaved) Lutheran, had given her heart to the Lord Jesus on New Year's Eve, just as I had on the same night some years ago, and also followed Him later on in baptism. Now we were truly one in Spirit, and together with Katitza we often had beautiful fellowship and prayer together.

# CHAPTER 13

# The Man Who Was Declared Dead

*For whether we live, we live unto the Lord; and whether we die, we die unto the Lord: whether we live therefore, or die, we are the Lord's. (Romans 14:8)*

Everyone in our church liked Gunter, who visited us about twice a month. We planned to get married the following year, but a motorcycle accident put him in the hospital with a complicated fracture of his left leg. We had to postpone the wedding date. I went to see him and stayed in his home for a few days. In this "leisure time" for Gunter, he finally shared a little more about his life.

Since early childhood he had helped in the bakery. At the age of ten he had to get up at 4

167

o'clock in the morning to help his father in the bakery.

"The first thing in the morning," he said, "my father would pray with me. He and Mother had come to know the Lord just a few years earlier, coming out of the Lutheran church. I also accepted Jesus as my Savior and was baptized on my profession of faith.

"After school I had to deliver bread on the bicycle with a big basket on the front. Once I had some bread to deliver for the mayor's wife. I rang the doorbell and as usual said, *'Gutentag;* here is the bread.'

"I was angrily interrupted. 'Don't you know that a German greets, "Heil Hitler"? You need not bring me any more bread.'

"When I told this to my father, he only said, 'That's OK. Don't worry about it.'

"My father wanted me to become a baker too, and I was sent to another baker in town to learn the trade. My master was in the NS and was very strict. He couldn't understand that I wanted to go to Bible study and prayer meeting on Wednesday and said, 'You're lying. No young boy goes where the old women sit,' but I went anyhow. I think the only time he went to church was for my funeral, the memorial service in our Christus Kirche."

"Tell me, Gunter, how did all this really happen to you?" I was eager to know.

"I was drafted at sixteen, first into the work-force, where we had to dig ditches and build roads, etc. A few months later I had to join the army. I almost ended up in the SS, Hitler's army.

"When we had to line up one day, a tall SS officer came to inspect us. With eyes like a hawk he pointed with his finger, 'You and you and you and you' at my comrades, all quite tall and strong, who had to leave and join the SS troops. I was quite sleepy that morning and must have looked pretty dumb. Thank God I was not chosen. We were all about sixteen or seventeen, the last hope of the army, and were trained by some experienced soldiers to handle a gun, to march, to obey.

"A few months later we were asked what we were most interested in. I chose to become a tank driver. We were sent to a military school in Straubing at the Donau, where we learned everything about a tank."

"That is quite interesting, Gunter," I said. "My brother Karl was also in Straubing when he was taught to become a fighter pilot. Maybe you were near him there."

"I remember them flying low over the Donau, doing their exercises," he answered. "But I was busy learning about tanks. Everything about a tank was quite interesting to me. My driver's training took about six weeks. We had to drive in the fields and all over the place; then we went into the real army.

"Four men were in the tank: the gunner, Paul; Siegfried, the radio man; the sergeant, Otto; and I, the driver. Sometimes when we had to wait or we were in a barrack, I had a chance to play my little mouth organ and we sang. They were special comrades to me and we became quite close, getting along well.

"First they sent us to the east front, but then they turned us around, put the tanks and us on trains and moved us toward the west front. Nobody really knew what was going on. To avoid bomb attacks the trains were hiding in the tunnels during the day and at night we went on.

"When we reached the west front, we were thrown into the last push of the army, the Battle of the Bulge in France. This was December 16, 1944. We were in this for two days. On December 18 our tank got hit by a grenade and caught fire. We all tried to escape. Someone was shooting at us with a machine gun. I was terrified. All of us ran toward a sandpit, with bullets flying around us. Then I made a mistake; I lay down—and someone shot me with a machine gun.

"First I was hit over both hands close to my face, then my left arm flew to the side and the next bullet landed in my chest right over my heart and went on into my arm. You know, it's strange—you just feel something very hot."

I had seen the big scars on Gunter's hands but never the one on his chest. A piece of muscle was missing, leaving a hole half an inch deep amid the scars.

"What happened then?" I asked. "How did you ever get through it?"

"My good friend Paul held me in his arms. I was bleeding heavily. 'You will take me home, Paul?' I asked.

"Yes," he said. "You are going home."

"I called out, 'My God, my God,' and 'Mother, Mother!' Then I passed out and Paul left me for dead. During the night I woke up a few times and fainted again, in between hearing the explosions and rumbling of tanks. I was in no-man's-land, where all the 'dead heroes' were lying. Toward morning I woke up. Because I had been doubled up on my side, the bleeding had clotted up and stopped. My hands, very swollen, were still in my gloves, which were soaked with blood. I stumbled ahead, not knowing where I was, not knowing where the enemy or any of our troops were."

I interrupted him. "Gunter," I said, "I am sure God put you in that doubled-up position to stop you from bleeding to death. God had His angels watching over you!"

"I know," he said, smiling. "But then I got stuck on some barbed wire and could not get loose. Still half in a trance, I finally got free and staggered on, right into a ditch. Three American soldiers were there in the trench.

"One of them came out and said, 'Come on, boy,' and he took me into the trench. He put some powder that looked like sugar all over my hands and the wounds on my chest, and then placed me on the hood of a jeep and drove me about 300 feet to a Red Cross tent, where there were doctors and nurses. I was so glad to be alive. The Lord was so good to me.

"There they fixed me up. They put my chest and both arms up to the elbow into a cast. They also stretched my fingers, since the middle hand bones were smashed. The pains were horrible, so they had to take some of the pins out of my fingertips. I was then transported from there to Lyson, into a field hospital.

"About thirty soldiers were in that tent with a potbellied stove in the middle that kept us fairly warm. In December France is not so cold. One day a male nurse came to my bed, and with a smile shoved something into my mouth. I didn't know what it was; I had never ever eaten peanut butter. I couldn't get it out *or* down! For a moment I thought I had gotten through the fighting only to choke on this strange, sticky food. The kind gentleman thought he did me a favor, but we don't grow peanuts in Germany!

"Then by Christmas they had transferred me to Paris into a big hospital. On Christmas Eve a French priest came to my bed.

"I said, *'Ich bin ein Baptist.'*

"He only heard 'Baptist' and turned around,

went out the door and got four American soldiers. They all were Baptists, and they brought me chocolate and candies and other things. We were brothers in the Lord. For us the war was finished, and together we celebrated the birth of our Lord and Savior, Jesus Christ. I will never forget their love—Christmas of 1944 in Paris. I wish that I could sometime meet any of these men again.

"In one of the hospitals there was a German doctor, Frau Wendt. She was on a Red Cross exchange program, and since I as a patient could not write a card to my parents, she offered to do this for me after she was released.

"My lieutenant, informed by my comrade Paul of my 'dying in his arms,' sent a consolation note and report of my death on the battlefield to my parents."

Gunter showed me both letters of the doctor and his lieutenant and continued, "My parents and family mourned for me for a few months. This is the memorial service they held for me in our church."

With tears in my eyes I read:

Memorial Service for Gunter Klinksiek
February 4, 1945
For whether we live, we live unto the Lord;
Or whether we die, we die unto the Lord:
Whether we live therefore, or die,
We are the Lord's.
Romans 14:8

And the song Gunter loved best was written out. It was a song I also knew from back home, with the beautiful bass solo accompanied by the choir and a refrain. It says:

Make me purer, make me smaller,
And my heart content in Thee,
You alone can give new life,
Lead me to eternity.

Make me purer, make me smaller,
Give me, Lord, a faithful heart;
Make me steadfast, You my all,
Draw my life and heart to Thee.

That night we sang it together with grateful hearts.

"How did your parents find out that you were alive?" I asked.

"My father got up one morning," Gunter continued, "and said, 'Mother, I had a dream. I saw Gunter sitting on a bed holding both hands up and saying, "Father, one day we will be baking together again." '

"Mother said, 'Hermann, you and your dreams. Don't say something like that. I'm just getting over it.' You know my mother is always a little harsh.

"The mail came as usual, but one day among the returned letters stamped with 'Died for great Germany' was a letter with strange handwriting, addressed to my parents. Mother opened it and read: 'I can tell you today that your son Gunter is alive and though wounded in his chest and both hands, he will be all right.'

"Here, you can read the letter for yourself." Gunter handed it to me.

I was so touched by God's grace and protecting love, bringing back the only son to his family, that I could say nothing.

"You can imagine," Gunter continued, "how the customers in the bakery rejoiced when my three sisters and my mother suddenly wore happy summer dresses instead of the black ones for mourning.

"Having been released as a patient from the hospital, I was then transferred to a prison camp near Cherbourg in France. It was a big field where a few hundred of us, surrounded by high barbed-wire fences, were trying to find a little hole in the ground to lie down. Seventeen of us men had to share one loaf of bread a day. Each one got a piece of chocolate, a cube of sugar and a little bit of dried tea with milk. I found an old can, stirred everything together with some water and added some edible weeds which grew near the fence. With dried grass I made a fire, and these things kept me alive.

"Then one day we were all loaded on a big troop transporter to go to a work camp in the United States. When we were halfway across the ocean, on May 6, 1945, the war ended, and we turned back to the prison in France.

"On July 8, 1945, we had to appear for a count. Everyone younger than eighteen and those over sixty-five was ordered to step out. We didn't know why, but then we were informed that we would be sent home. You can imagine how overjoyed we were.

"They drove us on big trucks to a release station in Minden, about twenty kilometers away from my hometown, Bad Oeynhausen. Someone recognized me on the truck and notified my father. When we arrived in Minden, he was already waiting there with his motorcycle and in his white baker's uniform."

"Oh, I can imagine what joy that was," I said. "I remember what it meant to me, being united with my family."

"Yes," Gunter agreed. "And you should have seen the man behind the desk when I went to apply for my food ration card. With big eyes, he looked over his glasses at me and down again at the canceling of my registration, with a mark 'deceased.' Shaking his head, he finally filled out a new registration form, believing that what he saw was real. . . . I *was* alive and sitting right in front of him.

"A year later a letter came from my good friend Paul, from East Germany, who apologized to my parents for not being able to put into words what had been weighing so heavily

on his heart. He wanted to give a truthful report of my last words and how I died in his
arms. You can imagine his joy when I myself
answered him, sending him a picture of me.
When he wrote me back, he said, 'Your picture
is under my Christmas tree.' Here, Magdalene,
read it yourself. Paul also has great faith in
God, having now seen His protecting love over
me. Despite the hard times there, he too will
hold on to his Lord."

I was looking at Gunter's scars again, particu-
larly the left hand, with the middle hand bone
so mangled, the shortened index finger hanging down limply, then the deep scar in his
chest. I shuddered.

"What a miracle that you are here!" I told
him. "God is so merciful! And then He brought
us both through the chaos of the last months of
this horrible war, each one alone! Yet God
never left us. His angels were watching over
you and me." Our hearts were so grateful to
our heavenly Father.

# CHAPTER 14

# Farewells

*Be strong and of a good courage; be not afraid, neither be thou dismayed: for the LORD thy God is with thee whithersoever thou goest. (Joshua 1:9)*

My father was retiring, and my parents moved into our apartment. It was so good to have them with me and with my grandparents, especially because I would have to leave them after the wedding. My parents settled in, and Papa got involved right away in our growing Baptist church. We started planning my wedding.

We were all shocked when Papa almost lost his life in a serious accident. Riding his bicycle to a Bible study out of town, he was struck by a car. He had a double concussion, and his pelvis and legs were broken. We could only thank the

Lord that he was still alive. Much prayer went up for him, and instead of amputating one leg, the surgeon was able save it, though it became two inches shorter than the other leg.

Gunter and I postponed our wedding date another six months. Finally Papa said in the spring of 1950, "Magda, by the 30th of April I should be out of the hospital. Go ahead with your plans."

He was soon out of the hospital, though still in a cast and not able to come to the church service. I will never forget the beautiful scene when my dear father came home and was carried up the three flights of stairs. Mama welcomed him with open arms. With joyful tears she said, "Now I have my dear husband back again. Thank You, Lord! Thank You, Lord!"

Knowing that there would be increasing responsibility on my shoulders, I was quite nervous and tense when I realized that I needed an operation on the tear duct of my eye four days before the wedding. After the operation I had to wear a black patch over my eye which the doctor hoped to remove the day before the wedding. I wondered if I would look like a pirate going down the aisle. So many times I just prayed, *Oh, Lord, see me through this. Give me strength.* And my faithful heavenly Father did give His grace.

Wearing a borrowed dress from a war widow but a lovely new veil through my Uncle Fritz's connections, I walked to the altar on the arm of my husband-to-be.

The choir sang the song I had so much wished for but had not expected they would be able to practice on their own:

> Make our home a hut of God,
> In friendliness with us abide.
> Oh, live with us in our midst,
> And we have endless happiness.
> And You, our daily blessed guest,
> Make our home a royal place.
>
> Where You are Lord, there's joyful living,
> And heaven's blessing blooming there.
> You're clothing us with silk and riches,
> Though this world sees a poorly dress.
> And this abundance never cease,
> While with such little we have peace.

This, my own wedding, was the very first one I had ever attended, and we had no rehearsal. Gertrud's daughter was our flower girl, and seeing her widowed mother cry, she grabbed my veil to wipe her own tears. It seemed to me like an omen. Would there be tears ahead of us?

---

My dearest wish was to start a family right away, and the Lord granted us this wish the following year. He gave us a healthy, strong eight-and-a-half-pound baby boy, Karl Gunter, born in February 1951. Though with great anticipation I had sewn his diapers, blankets and little shirts and read all about baby care in my big book, *The Woman as House Doctor*, I was overwhelmed with a mixture of indescribable happiness, gratitude and fear. How would I handle this strong little boy? It took me a while until I relaxed and he did too.

A year later in July 1952, the Lord gave us another healthy little boy, Peter, even bigger—nine-and-one-half pounds. Both boys had red-blond hair and were our great joy.

The bakery business in Gunter's parents' home involved six adults—everyone except Gunter's youngest sister, nine years old and, naturally, our little two boys. Not having our own household, at least we had a little living room and one bedroom upstairs.

The fellowship in Gunter's church was strengthening, and singing in the choir was a spiritual outlet for Gunter and me. Many people had to leave their homes and apartments because the military was still occupying their houses. Gunter's parents had offered to keep the piano of one family in their living room. To us this was the leading of the Lord.

Often on Sunday evenings young couples and friends from church came over for hours of singing and fellowship.

Our little family was growing, yet after three years we still did not have our own household. Though we had repeatedly applied to the town hall to rent the little apartment available across the street, the application was always denied. Millions of people had fled from the East to the West and were crowded together in houses, which often caused friction. There seemed to be no hope of getting out of our situation.

One day a letter came from my sisters Edith and Anneliese, who had immigrated to Detroit in the United States, where my Uncle Hans, Mama's half brother, and his family lived. They encouraged us to leave the overcrowded West Germany and immigrate to the US too.

Gunter's father was delighted, since his own wish as a young man had been to immigrate to that great new world. It had never come true for him, so he hoped to follow us one day. A Christian man named Karl Gunter and his family from a Baptist church in Cleveland, Ohio, sponsored us. They picked us because our little boy's name was Karl Gunter.

Yet God seemed to have other plans for us. When we were called to the American Consulate, we stood in a long line for hours. Then with just five people in front of us, we were told the quota to immigrate to the US was closed for that year.

The weeks and months that followed tested our trust and faith, but we knew that God was in control. And again in these months of transition I recognized God's clear direction: He opened the doors for us to immigrate to Canada. Unexpectedly Reverend Sturhahn, through the North American Baptist Conference, offered sponsorship for German Baptist refugees.

My sisters lent us the money for the long trip by boat, and on May 6, 1953, we left our former homeland of Germany, no longer able to provide room for a growing, young family. When we said goodbye to my parents, little Karl Gunter, then two years old, said to Mama, "*Oma, bis gleich*," which means, "See you in a little while."

And I hung onto these words. Maybe through God's will we would see each other again. I kept in my heart their last words, "The Lord be with you."

Gunter's mother was concerned that we would have nothing to eat over there, so she put a large ham and some smoked sausage in the bottom of the baby buggy in which our ten-month-old son Peter was laid.

On the sixteenth of May, after a stormy ten-day trip, we arrived in Halifax on the 17,000-ton ship, *Neptunia*. Someone mentioned that no meat was allowed to be brought into the country. I didn't know what to do, but I silently prayed while I pushed Peter's buggy down the ship's ramp. Gunter was behind me carrying Karl.

A Red Cross nurse met me at the foot of the ramp, and with a kind smile she took the buggy from my hands and pushed it past the customs officer. There she waited until our passports and papers were checked.

*So You, my Lord, are here already taking care of us,* I thought. *Thank You so much.*

We stopped at Quebec City, and then went on to Montreal where we were told, "This train ends here." As we stepped out, two women approached us with a smile. But with words we did not understand, they grabbed our little boys and took off. Holding onto our bags, bewildered, we rushed after them till they stopped and motioned us to follow them into a play room.

Seeing my questioning eyes, one explained in broken English, "We watch your babies, you look at the town. You have three hours' time." We had not ever experienced this kindness in our overcrowded Germany. Content that our boys were safe, we walked out of the station, being careful to remember every corner we turned. The signs at the street corners and the language people used was not English; this much I recognized. Then I remembered reading up on Canada. There was a French province, Quebec. We did not understand this language, but the kindness of the people touched our hearts.

Coming into a country so large staggered our

mind. How much space, how much freedom, how kind the people at the railroad station, looking after our children! We had never expected this.

Arriving in Windsor, Canada, the closest city to Detroit, we marveled at the tall skyline of this mighty city across the wide river. My sisters were waiting for us—oh, what joy! To see each other again after almost three years! It was so good not to be all alone. A very kind pastor, Jack Watts from the Fellowship Baptist Church, gave us a warm welcome. We were to stay in a furnished house with a German family who would soon move to the US. On the way there Pastor Watts picked up a bed for us. After a few days he found a job in a bakery for Gunter.

The German family we lived with had moved, so we were on our own. Every day Gunter took the bus to Windsor, about sixteen miles away from us. We were so glad to have our own household for the first time!

But it was only a few days later that a big van from Sears stopped in front of our house to pick up the furniture—which the people had not paid for.

Now Karlchen was sleeping on the floor, and we were sitting on our moving boxes. The future looked dim. My sisters would not be able to come until the next week on their days off, and we did not have their phone number or a phone of our own. Gunter's work week was over and his first paycheck was for $18, but our rent was $80. You don't need to speak good English to do arithmetic. This wouldn't work out for us! Then came a notice from the hydroelectric company to pay a $30 deposit to keep the water and electricity on. We saw ourselves in a hopeless situation.

*Oh, God,* I prayed, *what shall I do?*

My husband was frustrated, not understanding the language. Totally discouraged, he sat on the wooden crate that had carried our few precious belongings over the ocean, several thousand miles from his loved ones.

In such a situation homesickness takes over, whether one likes it or not. I set my little Peter in the buggy and sneaked out of the house.

*Oh, Lord,* I prayed again, *help me!*

At the utility office I got extended time for another week to pay the $30 deposit. Then I walked down to the highway. I felt very weak, my arm still being very badly infected from a vaccination required to enter Canada. Trembling with fatigue, I reached the phone booth. As I stood dialing Pastor Watts' number and holding on to the buggy with my happy little boy rocking in it, I felt myself growing faint.

"Hello?" I heard Pastor Watts on the other end.

My voice was faint. "We need you, Pastor, and oh, God help me, my baby!" With those words, I blacked out.

When I regained consciousness, I had slid
to the floor of the phone booth, and Peter's
buggy had rolled down the hill and come to a
halt at the shoulder of the highway, Peter still
happily rocking in it. Hysterically crying and
barely able to walk, I took my child to the little variety store a few yards away. Someone
brought me a glass of water while I sat on
some empty Coca-Cola boxes, trying to get
my composure back. Walking home very
slowly to gain more time so my husband
would not see my tears and be worried, I
thanked my Lord for the angels who had
watched over our little boy.

I was barely home, sharing the good news
that the payment of the deposit had been extended for another week, when the doorbell
rang.

There stood Pastor Watts, who had guessed
what had happened to me. With the compassion of Christ, he put his arm around me, comforting us and assuring Gunter that he would
look for another job for him. Through a member of his church, Gunter got into the Chrysler
Corporation.

I remembered Romans 8:28: "And we know
that all things work together for good to them
that love God, to them who are called accord-
ing to his purpose." God heard my cry. He
knew of our needs and was with us, and that
was all that mattered.

We now had $69 a week and new hope in our hearts. Yet Gunter was using fifty cents daily for the bus ride to town and our rent was still $80 plus expenses for our large unfurnished home. We started to look through the ads of our neighbor's newspaper. Then my eyes stopped. There was a Steinway upright piano for sale for $75. We both knew that was for us, paying it off at $15 a week. What joy filled our hearts when five young German men from the church helped Gunter carry that heavy old black instrument into our little living room. One day a man who worked with Gunter at Chrysler visited us with his wife.

"That's interesting," he said. "No table, no chairs, but a piano and stool."

"Oh," I laughed. "You see, one could eat on it, sit on it, lie on it; but really we only love to play it."

---

By now I was expecting my third child. Edith, on her day off, went with Gunter to look at a little house downtown in Windsor. It was a tiny house with one bedroom, a living room, dining room and kitchen, but it was furnished and a place to stay for the winter—which we did. It was close to the Campbell Baptist Church, where Pastor Watts preached, and there we felt right at home. Though I could understand only a little of the English and Gunter none, the songs often had the same melodies as ours in Germany.

We met some young German immigrants there. In the evening after church they loved to come to our little house to sing our old familiar youth and choir songs. How good that felt, the fellowship in Jesus Christ! With the German youth group from the North American Baptist Church coming over from Detroit and Reverend Patzia from Richmond Baptist in Detroit, we started evening services in the YMCA.

———————

In November Gunter got sick from riding his bike through the cold, moist air, and a few days later he was laid off. We didn't know at that time what "layoff" meant. This happened just before he was to get his seniority, and because of that he would get no unemployment compensation.

*Lord, what now?* I prayed. *We need You.* I felt led to take the bike and ride to Chrysler. I asked for the foreman. "Sir, why did you fire my husband? He is sick and cannot come to work. The doctor said he has rheumatic fever."

The man looked at me. *Perhaps he does not understand my accent,* I thought. I repeated my question, praying not to show tears.

"Wait a moment," he said, taking my name and address. "We'll send a nurse."

God had arranged all this. Since we would get no unemployment, now we would get sick benefits of $32, which was four dollars more than the $28 of unemployment. Advent came and our young people from church came again to visit and sing in our tiny little house. As they left they handed us a Christmas card, and in it was $75—enough to pay the December rent of $50 plus some other bills. Oh, how we thanked the Lord! We knew He would carry us through.

Christmas Eve came. With only two dollars left, I bought a fifty-pound bag of potatoes for seventy-five cents. Pushing it home on the bicycle, there at the street corner I saw some Christmas trees. Maybe I could get one for a dollar or less! But I would also need a pair of mittens; my fingers were always getting so cold. I wondered what to do.

But then I thought of the box of pretty Christmas tree ornaments we had brought from Germany. My decision was made, and I found the cheapest tree available. I joyfully carried my surprise home and saw that our screen door was half open. There was a brown paper parcel in between the doors. What could that be?

My eyes got big when I found a large chicken in that parcel, no name signed. God had moved someone's heart to bring us this gift. I cooked the bones over and over again for soup, and that chicken lasted almost from

Christmas till New Year's. The gifts my sisters brought for the children brought much joy. I got a scarf and the much-needed mittens. Uncle Hans and Aunt Frieda also visited us in the holidays and brought us a big basketful of fruits and the traditional turkey. We felt like royalty—and why not? Deep inside we knew: We were the children of the King of kings!

---

When spring came, Gunter was better but not yet back to work. My sisters helped with the rent during these months, but on one day there was no bread in the house and still some time until one of them would come on her day off. I prayed that morning, *Lord, You know I have no bread for today and no money to buy some.* Karl Gunter, playing in front of the house, suddenly came running in. "Mommy, Mommy, *Der Hottemax hat ein Brot verloren*—The horsie has lost a bread."

Astonished, I went outside. There, half a block down the street, went a horse-drawn bread wagon, one side of the back door still swinging open. Realizing that the bread must have fallen out in front of our house, I said, "Karlchen, our dear God let us have this bread today."

A few days later I received an invitation from a lady in our church. She picked me up in her car and took me to her house. Upon entering, I saw several ladies already sitting there beside a basket full of gifts.

I apologized, "I am sorry; I did not know there was a birthday. I brought no gift." I felt terrible.

They all smiled. Someone said, "No, this is a shower for you." I was led to the chair beside the table. I still wasn't sure what was going on when they asked me to open a gift. It contained a lovely baby jacket. Then I realized that these were parcels of love for my first baby on this continent—it was my baby shower. I had never heard about this beautiful custom before. When they took me home, the car was loaded with many beautiful things for our first baby to be born in Canada. Still in a dream, Gunter and I looked at these beautiful gifts given to us with so much caring Christian love. There were lovely baby clothes, plus bottles, diapers, blankets and all I needed so much. The garments I had sewn for our first child were worn out by the second one. A fresh joy came into our hearts, thinking of our third child, due to come in six or seven weeks.

We had been in this country almost a year but had not yet visited my uncle and aunt in Detroit. With permission granted at the customs office, Edith took me over the border. During my first time on American soil there at my aunt's house, I met her family and was once more surprised with a shower for our baby to come.

I stayed overnight and almost had my first sweet little baby girl in the United States. But she arrived the next day, March 20, 1954, six weeks too early.

I woke up that morning as my water broke. That afternoon our neighbor took me to the hospital. The procedure was quite different here in North America than in Europe. I received a little anaesthetic, which I never had with our boys, who were both delivered by midwives. In Europe only abnormal pregnancies required a visit to a doctor, so I had no prenatal care.

As I awoke from the anaesthetic I heard the nurses whisper in surprise. Margaret Ortud, premature and only five pounds, six ounces, needed special care.

A blood clot developed in my left leg and I had to stay longer. The next day when the doctor visited he mentioned that in his thirty years as a doctor he had never seen a baby as thin as a notepad, and it was a little boy. With his thick Hungarian accent he was barely understandable.

When I was released I had not yet seen my little girl, thinking I was not allowed to. But two weeks passed and my longing for her became unbearable. I went to the neighbor (we had no phone) to call the doctor, who told me I was permitted to visit her in the premature ward.

When Edith and Anneliese came to visit, they took me to the hospital. How tiny Margaret was! But the movement in her skinny little arms and legs was quite lively.

On the day when she finally came home, I heard Anneliese say to Gunter, "Wouldn't it have been nice if the little boy would have lived." My heart almost stopped.

"What do you mean?" I asked.

"Didn't you know you had twins, but the other little one died?"

My mind raced back to the remark my doctor had made—but I didn't want to think about it. I had my sweet little blond Margaret in my arms, and that was all that mattered. God had kept me from carrying my pregnancy to term because it could have been very dangerous for me.

We had to keep Margaret warm with the temperature over eighty degrees. That little gas heater in the living room burned day and night, and it was not long until we smelled gas throughout the house. When we had it checked out, we were told we had leaky pipes under the house. I had also noticed a crack in the baseboard where the sun was shining through, and when I washed the floors the water ran in one direction on the badly slanted floor. The big tree in front must have lifted the front section of the old wood duplex where we lived. We were quite concerned and knew we would have to move out before winter. But we knew that God was aware of all of this.

It was a beautiful spring afternoon, and I went around the duplex house to take my laundry off the line, all the pretty things I was so proud of. Some towels and Gunter's shirt were hanging there—but all my baby laundry was gone. I knew I had hung it all up, but there was nothing there! I was baffled.

Then I remembered that while I was hanging up my laundry in the morning, a woman was going down the alley with an empty old baby buggy. Could she have taken it? I was numb and puzzled at the same time. But a second thought came to me, as if God had gently said, *That mother was desperate and needed it.* I knew that I had enough clothes for my little baby since I had been given two showers. God was there, and He knew what I needed.

---

# CHAPTER 15

# The Lord's Way with Houses

*Be careful for nothing; but in every thing by prayer and supplication with thanksgiving let your requests be made known unto God. (Philippians 4:6)*

Gunter came home one day with the news that a coworker had a house for rent. We looked at it and loved it right away.

It had a little garden with an apple tree. Our heavenly Father had everything prepared for us already. The house was partly furnished, and soon we could afford our first kitchen table set and bunk beds for our two boys. Times were getting better.

I now had three German piano students and one adult student, Lisel Miller, who became a very dear friend to me. Though single she was like a second mother to our children.

Now that we lived outside the city we would need a car. Again God supplied. A couple from our church moved to the US and offered us their car for a low price. Doesn't God's Word say in Isaiah 65:24: "And it shall come to pass, that before they call, I will answer; and while they are yet speaking, I will hear"? A year later we drove back to see the old duplex, but we couldn't find it. The place had become a parking lot.

In July 1954 the Lord sent us a German-speaking pastor, Gerhart Schroeder, to serve our little group since we had some older people who understood only their mother tongue. I joyfully accepted the position as pianist. A beautiful fellowship grew among the young people, who were often in our home for Saturday evening meetings. All of us had lost everything as refugees and had started life afresh in a new homeland, though we came from different parts of Europe: Poland, Russia, Hungaria, Yugoslavia—and Danzig. We all loved to sing our special German hymns. And so we were united as a real, international, German-speaking church, with one leader, our Lord Jesus Christ.

We enjoyed our little growing family so much. Every time I held my newborn in my arms, a prayer of praise and thanksgiving went up to my heavenly Father for His marvelous, wonderful gifts of grace, so healthy and so beautifully formed.

How kind our God is to listen to our little prayers! If the answers are in His plan, He will give us the desires of our heart. In July 1956 He answered my prayer for another girl—a beautiful, healthy baby girl was laid into my arms, nine pounds and nine ounces, Giselle Susan, with gorgeous red hair. The crib in which we laid our first child in Germany was still doing its work in Canada. Over the crib hung a framed verse I had written in Gothic script letters with red ink on soft blue paper. Translated it reads:

> Out of God's hand
> You, my child, have come.
> Out of God's hand I received you, little one,
> Out of God's hand.
>
> Into God's hand
> Do I lay you again.
> You, the living blessing of love,
> Not in vain
> Into God's hands.
>
> From this, God's hand,
> I know without doubt,
> That you, my darling,
> No one can take out
> From this, God's hand.

Gunter's father's long-harbored wish was finally fulfilled when he and Gunter's mother and younger sister Erika immigrated to Canada six weeks after our Giselle Susan was born. It was so beautiful for the children finally to have Opa and Oma Klinksiek with us, and I had my very first week of vacation.

With only two bedrooms, we had to look for another, larger house and soon found one, again half-furnished. We two families split the $100 rent, and all looked well for three months.

Then came the big layoff at Chrysler, and at the same time the chance for Gunter's father to rent a little bake shop and move into an apartment nearby. With $28 unemployment we could no longer afford the rent. We had four weeks to move out and find another place. But who would take a family with four children and the father without work in the wintertime? Only God could do a miracle for us. I laid this matter before Him.

One week went by and nothing happened. Taking our boys' Sunday school teacher, my friend Anni, home for dinner, I shared my concern with her.

"Why don't you buy a house rather than rent one?" she asked.

"With what?" was my reply. "We have no savings."

The next day Anni called. "Magdalene, I was

praying for your situation, and the Lord just told me, 'You have $700 in the bank. You could lend it to them to buy a house.' "

This was far above all our expectations, but I continued trusting my Lord that He would guide us further if He really wanted us to have a house of our own in such critical times.

Then the Lord brought the name of the German real estate man to my mind, the one who had dealt with our church building sale. I told him our situation and that we had only three weeks left to find a place.

"Mrs. Klinksiek, this looks quite hopeless now in the wintertime and with only $700 borrowed money," he said.

"Mr. Graef," I replied, "you don't know that I have a strong faith in God. I believe that He will let you find a place."

Less than a week later he called back. "This is very unusual, but a German man who is also laid off at Chrysler already has his visa to move to join his brother in the US. He and his wife want to meet you." Entering an older house, my eyes fell on the German meditation calendar on the wall.

"You are Christians!" I said.

"Yes, we are," they smiled.

"And we are too," we replied, realizing that God had been surely at work. Both their prayers and ours were answered.

My obedient sister in Christ, Anni, had also

lost everything as a refugee, but God had planned that she use her savings for us. The owners settled for that down payment, and God had even more in store for His trusting children. The man who left asked if his wife and two children could remain six weeks on the upper floor, which had all the necessities, allowing us to have our first two months free. With our few things we moved into the two large rooms and the big kitchen downstairs.

We put the bunk beds for the boys in the dining area of the kitchen with a curtain for privacy in front of it. We ourselves slept with the girls in the dining room and still had the living room for all of us. The owner of the house, Mr. Eshker, left all his furniture behind, giving us a whole year to pay it off at a reasonable price.

But since we had no more than $28 to $32 unemployment a week and $60 mortgage to pay, plus water and gas, there was little left for food. Many people in our city were unemployed, but there were several small factories on our street. I tried to coax Gunter to look for a job. "Anything!" I said. "Just so we have a little more to survive."

But he hesitated to go, and I became more and more frustrated. Finally one afternoon after I had tried to encourage him again, almost losing my patience, he left the house, not saying a word. I watched him from the front window as he walked slowly down the street. My heart was heavy. *Oh, Lord, help him.*

After an hour passed by, I saw him coming through the gate at the alley as if carrying a heavy load.

"Did you have any success?" I asked hopefully.

No answer. No matter how I tried, there was only silence.

The next day I realized there was something wrong that I could not understand. After some gentle persuading, he finally shared one of his fears. He did not want to ask for a job that required knowledge of a language he did not speak or understand. At Chrysler a German-speaking man, Ernst Herman, who became Gunter's friend, was his interpreter, explaining to him the work procedures on the line.

But speaking our mother tongue at home and at church gave him little opportunity to learn the English language. I had never thought of this, having taken six years of English in high school and being able to speak and understand much of the language. I realized then that the Lord expected me to take over some unwanted and unexpected responsibilities. God was faithful, giving me continual help and wisdom as we adapted to our new land.

By the time the family upstairs left, we knew why the Lord had them stay. We had learned to manage with the rooms downstairs and a bathroom with a shower in the basement. We could now rent out the upstairs, which would pay the $60 mortgage. We fixed it up as pretty as possible.

One day we were eating dinner in the kitchen, laughing and carefree as we watched little Susan making funny faces. The doorbell rang. *Maybe someone saw the apartment-for-rent sign in the window*, I thought. Gunter opened the front door. A young couple wanted to see the rooms, so Gunter took them upstairs.

I prayed a short, *Oh, Lord, let them like it—and keep the children quiet.* But again Susan caused them to laugh.

"What did they say?" I asked Gunter when he returned to the table.

" 'It is nice' and 'Thank you.' They've left already."

I went to the window and saw them walking on the other side of the street. I pleaded, *Oh, Lord, she looked so kind. But You know best.*

The doorbell rang again. It was the same young couple.

"We talked it over," the man said. "My wife likes it here."

Some weeks later I asked the young French woman, Dorelda, "What made you come back here again?"

With tears in her eyes she smiled. "The happy laughter in this house," she said in broken English. "I come from New Brunswick and

I have eight younger brothers and sisters whom I miss so much."

---

Though there were two houses close beside us, an alley in the back and factories across the road, I marveled at how beautifully that little back yard blossomed in springtime. A rose gate led to an area where gooseberry and red currant bushes and a cherry tree stood, along with a sandbox and a swing set. Many flowers came up at the side of the fence, which was loaded with little climbing roses that bloomed profusely in June, hanging over to both sides for a private shelter. Our neighbors, an older couple, offered their plums to me to can, and again and again we saw God faithfully leading us through.

We had no luxuries, but we could have oatmeal in the morning and one hot meal at night. That kept us going, though I was told by the school nurse that the children looked under-nourished and I was underweight. We should eat more fruit and have vitamins and minerals, she said. I knew all that, but I knew that a time would come when we could have these things again, and the Lord knew it too.

I saw Him providing beautifully for our clothing when Edith, who took care of three little girls in a wealthy family in Detroit, brought loads of expensive dresses for our two girls every year. Up to age ten they were dressed like little princesses. Even I was dressed in costly gifts from the mother of these girls. I thought of one verse of our wedding song: "You're clothing us with silk and riches, though this world sees a poorly dress."

Times were hard all over in Windsor and the entire province of Ontario, and many from our church moved to Detroit and other cities, but the Lord saw us through. A great joy let us look ahead to the spring of 1960: My beloved parents would come to visit us. The children were excited, and I could hardly contain myself. Gunter and I drove to New York. Waiting there at the pier, my eyes searching the ramp where the passengers came down, I saw only my father.

I asked, "Gunter, do you see Mama?"

"No," he said.

"But where is Mama?" I got more anxious. My heart seemed to stop. Papa came closer, clearing his passport at the customs office . . . and still no Mama. Finally I reached him.

"Where is Mama?" I cried.

"She had to stay behind. She fell and broke her hip just before we boarded the ship. She was taken to the hospital in Celle with the Red Cross van. The brothers and sisters there will look after her, but I had to come alone. Our luggage and the big hi-fi stereo system for you had already gone through the office and been stored in the ship. It could not be canceled, so here I am, only half of us two."

Joy mingled with pain in my heart as we took my father to our waiting children. Often I went to the closet to hug my mama's dresses, hiding my tears in them, pretending she was close to me. But the next year God would make it possible for me to take our girls, Margaret, then six years old, and Susan, four, to see their Oma Krüger in Germany.

Papa saw that the time had come to give up his position as elder of the Baptist church in Celle to one of his younger deacons. With the help of the Lord and their church family, they immigrated to Canada in 1962. How we welcomed them with open arms! All was well now—and Gunter was never again laid off at Chrysler.

It was the next spring that my parents wanted to buy a lovely little house, and Papa and I tried to set it up comfortably for Mama.

I had a chance to start a part-time job and went through the training as a medical technician in Detroit. But I fainted once in a while and experienced light flashes in the right side of my field of vision. The examination for my working visa in Detroit showed a dark spot in my head— perhaps a tumor. I had to go through tests and got very bad side effects, which put me into the hospital twice that year for four to six weeks. There I lay, my head low and my feet high to ease the horrible headaches that made me faint as soon as I tried to sit up.

*Why did this have to happen to me?* I pondered. I thought I had managed so well; everything came so easy to me. I looked forward to my work with people. *Could it be that the Lord is saying "no" to my getting seriously involved in something else but music?* I thought. They held the position of medical technician open for me until August, but I had to go back into the hospital for another four weeks. Later I concluded that the Lord had limited my health so I would only be able to take care of my own family and take part in a few church activities.

⚬⚬⚬⚬⚬

In the spring of the following year, I walked to the corner store under a beautiful sky—filled with smelly factory air.

I looked up and prayed, *Oh, Lord, You know how much I love Your creation. Is it possible that one day You could let us live out of town, away from the factories and alley life?*

A few weeks later my parents' neighbor called early in the morning—Mama was ill. We rushed over and knew she had to get medical attention. From then on her problems got worse and worse. Mama was not able to speak a word of English, and her mind got quite confused when she was alone, though she let us know she was ready to go if this was God's will.

One morning my Aunt Frieda came to visit Mama. "Magda," she said, "I will take care of your mother today. You might want to do something for yourself."

"Yes," Papa answered for me, "I would like to plant a little peach tree. We should buy one today."

I didn't know where to buy one and looked in the yellow pages. "Klink's Nursery, North Talbot Road," I read. *Well,* I thought, *that sounds a little bit like Klinksiek. Let's see where that is.*

We found it a little distance outside of town. Turning into the road I said, "Papa, what a quiet area. Isn't this beautiful, so peaceful? There's even a meadow with cows over there—and these houses on the left are so far apart, such big properties," I bubbled. "Look! There's a house for sale. It looks a little bit like ours in Danzig with the gables." A faint thought came to my heart: *Maybe that could be ours. Oh, no.* I pushed the thought away. *That can't be.*

We purchased the peach tree in the nursery right beside that large property, which was separated from the nursery by a tall cedar tree hedge. The next day when I saw my father again at the hospital, I said, "Papa, I still think of that lovely house and that peaceful road."

"I was thinking of it, too," he said.

The coming Sunday afternoon I asked Gunter to take us all for a ride. "Stop right here," I said. "Do you see that house?"

"Yes. Why?"

"I feel in my heart that it is supposed to become our house."

He looked at me in unbelief. "You're crazy. How could that be?"

"I don't know, but that's how I feel. I prayed once for a place out of town, in the country," I replied, writing the phone number down. I got an appointment with the real estate agent, and Papa went with me to see it. I got out of the car and just stood there. The white Cape Cod was nestled among lots of bushes and big old trees on about half an acre of soft, rolling lawn, bordered by a long stretch of unworked field. I saw fruit trees, grapevines and raspberry rows in the distance. I took a few steps onto the green, springy lawn. "Look, Papa, there are some peonies coming up—and so many lilac trees!" It was all separated from the property to the left by a little creek and a bridge.

There were no houses in the back, just a fruit orchard as far as my eyes could see. *How beautiful that must be*, I thought, *when the trees are in bloom*. I had a vision of what this place would become if God wanted us to have it.

"Don't you want to see the house?" the real estate man asked.

"Oh, yes," I answered, interrupted in my thoughts. An older lady opened the door.

"Come in," she said in a friendly voice.

Walking through the house I saw an open Bible in the living room. My first question was once again, "You are a Christian?"

"Yes, my dear. I am a Baptist."

"So am I," I said.

And while the real estate man walked to the dining room, I whispered, "I love this place, but we really have no money."

"Oh," she said, "that is no problem. We will pray about it. If the Lord wants you to have it, you will get it."

Later on she told me that when she had watched me through the window, my eyes turning only to the big back yard, she had known I would love gardening, and for that she prayed.

The price was $21,000 with a $7,500 down payment. The real estate man looked quite pityingly at me when I told him that at this time we had no money for a down payment, but that I would call him back. A friend advised me to talk to the bank manager where we paid our $60 mortgage and explain the situation. He asked an employee for our account files.

"Sir," I said, "we have only $15 in that account."

"What does your husband earn?"

"About $90 a week."

"Do you work?"

"Yes, I earn about $7 a week; I have seven piano students. But I know we will be able to do it." Then I shared with him that I had prayed that our children would be able to grow up in a better neighborhood, a little way from town. "I believe that God has led me to this house," I finished.

He listened quietly and said, "I will think it over. Call me back after 1 o'clock."

I went home and got on my knees. *Lord, if it is Your will that we should have that place, let the man agree to it or give me grace to wait patiently.*

I called right after 1 o'clock.

"Mrs. Klinksiek, you and your husband can come to see me when he comes from work. We will give you the loan."

Gunter could not believe his ears when I said, "We have to go to the bank right away! They will give us the loan." And again we saw God's faithful leading through the next weeks of transition. The real estate man only shook his head when I told him how we got it.

Mama had lost more weight, and I had asked the doctor to let her come home to her own surroundings. She got stronger again, to the amazement of her doctor, but the traveling back and forth to look after their household and ours was getting quite hard for me. So the next year we got another loan to build an addition, with Papa taking responsibility to pay it off.

We planted many evergreens and different shapes of flower beds and even built a fish pond on the new 400-foot lawn. The Lord blessed our work.

My mother, sitting on the kitchen bench, looking at the beautiful private backyard, said, "Magda, you know this is close to paradise."

The whole family got involved in our house. Papa looked after our bunnies and vegetables; Mama visited the flower beds and watched the goldfish in the pond. The children helped by cutting the lawn and painting the house, which needed a total overhaul outside and inside.

I still remember the day I had picked the rows of strawberries and looked up to see the raspberries getting ripe also. *Oh, Lord, how good You are to us.* And walking back to the house, a real feeling of being home settled in my heart for the first time since Danzig.

# CHAPTER 16

# My World
# Falls Apart

*But God is faithful, who will not suffer you
to be tempted above that ye are able; but will
with the temptation also make a way to escape, that ye may be able to bear it. (1 Corinthians 10:13)*

That winter I started piano-teaching
courses in Detroit and soon started my
own music studio in our home. I was also busy
chauffeuring the children to their different
schools and music practices.

Gunter and I had our dreams set for them.
How proud I had been when they had played a
string quartet at the golden wedding anniversary of Mama and Papa a few years earlier! I
was now quite involved and always attended

their lessons to help with the technical aspect of their instruments. With all my strength I was determined to manage this growing family. Yet once in a while a strange feeling, a mixture of pride and fear, crept up in me. *I hope everything is going to be well.*

The influence of the late '60s and early '70s on the teenagers scared me. Anxiously Gunter and I continued our strict rules for our children, for home and church, with even more firmness.

Our last family camping vacation in Meaford, in the summer of 1969, ended with Gunter's desire to start a bakery business, which was for sale in the little town near the campground. I was confused about this, yet I did not want to be in his way as he wanted to get out of the factory life and be on his own.

Lying awake in the tent that night I prayed, *Oh, God, everything gets so confusing. I don't know what to do anymore. Please help us.* I had not prayed like that for some years. We had become so busy and independent. Frantically I had tried to keep our family devotions up, but to no avail. I myself often took little more time than five minutes to read my Bible, and that not even regularly.

Yet it seemed that God had heard my prayer and opened every necessary door for us. Everything seemed to fall into place. We had no problem getting the loan for the bakery, a beau-

tiful house near a stream to rent for a very reasonable price and even a little house for my
parents nearby. For the length of six weeks we
had a successful bakery business and put our
house in Windsor up for sale.

As if I were not part of all this, I drove the 250
kilometers back home every weekend after five
days' hard work to look after the girls, who had
stayed with my parents, and to do my church
duties.

On the day the realtor had open house for
our property, not one person showed up. The
real estate man, Mr. Graef, sat underneath the
big maple tree, watching me walk through the
backyard, trying to keep my tears back.

My mother was not feeling well, and the
next day Karl was supposed to move the first
furniture out, but the axle of the U-Haul
broke. As God had opened doors, so He
closed them again. Mama's condition wors-
ened. I called Gunter and told him what was
going on.

"The business is less than half since the tourists left," he said. "I've lost twenty-five pounds
in this short time. Call the real estate man and
see if he will take the contract back, and get me
the number of the Chrysler plant."

*Oh, God, help us through. Do what is best for all
of us,* I prayed again.

Gunter, having quit at Chrysler to start the
bakery, was told to be back in five days and he

would get his seventeen years of seniority back. Mr. Graef drew back the contract without charging us a penny.

"You know, Mrs. Klinksiek, I had prayed that no one would come to buy your place. You are meant to stay here," he said.

I realized that Mama was not getting better. A few days before that, she had said to me, "Magda, pray that the Lord takes me home. No one knows how much I suffer."

I went downstairs into the laundry room. *Oh, God,* I prayed, *I cannot do this. You know how much I love my mother, but You know how her condition is. If You want to take her home, give me strength.* In the three days that followed she was as sweet as ever.

Around this time she was concerned that she had not done enough for her Lord, and I reminded her of the grace of God she was saved by, and that that grace was still sufficient. Now the Lord Himself showed her that He had done everything.

"Come here," she said the next day, holding my hand tightly. "Promise me that you will take care of Papa as long as he lives. It will not be easy; he has his set ways, but don't ever leave him."

I promised.

That night our son Karl played his classical guitar for her. I sat at her bed. "Sing for me," she said.

I sang, "Fairest Lord Jesus" and other songs she loved so much. I sang the words to the song *"Jesus est der Schönste Name"*:

Jesus is the most beautiful name,
Above all names on earth.
Nothing can compare with Him,
And the glory is all His.

With her eyes resting on my lips, she whispered, "Let me rest in that name." Then her eyes opened again, trying to remember something, and she lifted her arm as if conducting a rhythm, trying to whisper some words.

I said, "Mama, do you mean,

Oh, You Lamb of God,
You have on Golgatha
Achieved the victory.
Amen, Hallelujah"?

Nodding her head, she continued,

"Nothing that I can bring,
He's done it all.
It is finished,
It is finished."

She seemed to fall asleep, but suddenly she tried to sit. Papa and I held her up.

"Mama?" she asked, which is what she called

my Oma. Looking straight ahead, she asked, "Who is that man?"

Papa said, "She sees her mother and her father, who died when she was a baby."

Then with wide-open eyes and an expression of great astonishment and wonder she breathed, "The High Priest." Gently we laid her back, and a few minutes later her soul had departed from us. Jesus Christ her Savior and faithful High Priest Himself ushered her into His glorious eternity. She saw what she believed.

Never could I forget these beautiful moments of Mama's homegoing, and I shared with many this experience that I had been so afraid to live through. God is so merciful, leaving us with memories to recall and to comfort us, that one day we will be with Him and our loved ones.

After my mama's funeral I put an ad in the *Toronto Star*, and the bakery was sold within two weeks. Everything was taken care of in short time. Even the lawyer who handled the transactions of buying and selling the bakery never sent us a bill.

---

But at home our four children, who had been active in our church choir and young people's group all these years, increasingly drew back from church life, which was still held in the German language and seemed not to feed their spiritual needs.

What do we do when childhood starts to fall off our children like the shell of a chestnut and the hard core of maturity becomes exposed? Do we try to keep the protective shell around our children when they pass through adolescence? These are most delicate, tender years and need much prayer and God's wisdom every day— but my own relationship with God at this time was about nil.

A growing fear made me feel almost numb. When all our children came into their teenage years together, I did not want to admit to myself that they would come under the influence of our times. Their involvement in church life, choir and youth group would keep the shell around them—I hoped. Our position in leadership of several church organizations just did not allow our children to miss a service or choir practice; pride did not let our "good reputation" be at stake.

The streets in the summers of the 1970s were lined with young hitchhikers trying to see the world. Our oldest son and a friend tried this adventure. Through his exciting letters, we followed him all through the beautiful West of Canada.

But we were not excited at all when soon a second of our children claimed that same freedom. Anxiety and fear gripped my heart; the weeks passed by and Gunter and I had no idea where this child was. My mind was trapped in imagining horrible situations coming true. Finally during one sleepless night when my heartache seemed unbearable, I called out, *Oh, God, I can't take it anymore—help me!*

There was silence first—would God hear me? But I hung on, and then came His answer: *Cast all your burdens on Him.*

*Lord, do You really mean this?* I prayed. *Then please take it all. I can't handle this anymore.*

It was as if a thousand pounds were lifted off my heart. Tears of relief ran down my cheeks onto my pillow.

The next day a letter came, relieving my greatest fear. We finally knew where our beloved child was. God had already worked ahead of my prayer, knowing that I would finally trust my child to Him. For the first time in weeks I felt peace in my heart. *He* was watching, guiding and teaching this child.

---

Never will I forget the day when our teenager who had wanted his freedom came home. Remembering that we ourselves could come back into the arms of our heavenly Father, we held our arms wide open as our prodigal walked into the house. With tears in our eyes we could only say, "We love you."

So often since then have I been reminded of that situation, for many times I have had to return to my Lord, confessing, *Lord, forgive me my*

*willfulness, making my own decisions, trying to
walk on my own way, not asking for Your will.*
Again and again His arms were wide open to
receive this prodigal, lovingly restoring me to
walk on with Him.

It takes all of a mother's strength to deliver a
sweet, God-given baby, carried nine months
close to her heart, into a strange, often abusive
and hostile world. Yet it seems so much harder
to give that same child, who stays all his life in
her heart, back into the wise and loving hands
of God. All four of my children had accepted
Jesus as their Savior, but I had forgotten that
God's grace was able to keep those who were
*also* His children. He loved them more than I
ever could, for He paid for them with His own
blood. But I had forgotten my teens when He
was so close to me, a refugee, all on my own.
My eyes were blinded. I looked only at the
dangerous circumstances.

As I looked back I realized that I had not
done what I had intended to do when I hung
the prayer poem over the crib of each newborn
and promised:

> Into God's hand do I lay you again,
> You, the living blessing of love not in vain,
> Into God's hand.

In that time Satan tried to get at my weak
spots: my fear, self-determination, worrying

and pride—and our good reputation. I did not know anything at that time about resisting the devil or spiritual warfare; I was eager to manage everything on my own. Unconciously I did what the devil tells us to do: "You can do it. You'll see—try a little harder." This is one of his old lies, sprouting from the root of pride. If it had not been for God's patience with this stubborn, self-sufficient mother, teaching me to surrender each child into His hand, I would not have survived those years.

And God continued to test my trust. It was the next Sunday when I felt a great restlessness in my heart. After dinner at home I withdrew to a quiet room. I had to do something; I could not pray, but I wrote down in a letter to God what I could no longer keep in my heart.

In quietness and in the light of God, I realized what I had done wrong in the past. In overprotecting my children, I tried to form their lives. Instead of talking so much, I should have prayed more for them and then left it up to God. I saw that others weren't made to please me, but to please God. I asked God's forgiveness for my wrong attitude and asked for His strength to help me not to mold my children after my wishes, but after His—not to *talk* about the life of the Christian, but to *live* it. *Jesus, help me to be more gentle and loving, less touchy and commanding. . . .*

Just as I wanted to put this little letter away,

my eyes fell on a little stationery card which
said:

> Lord, for tomorrow and its needs I do not
>     pray;
> Keep me, my God, from stain of sin, just
>     for today.
> Now set a seal upon my lips, for this I
>     pray;
> Keep me from wrong or idle words, just
>     for today.
> Let me be slow to do my will, prompt to
>     obey,
> And keep me, guide me, use me, Lord,
>     just for today.

And I wrote underneath, "Thank You, Lord."
On the page inside it said: "The LORD will per-
fect that which concerneth me" (Psalm 138:8). I
was overwhelmed at how faithful the Lord's
answer was to me. Even though I felt so inse-
cure and helpless as I tried to come close to
Him again, I knew it was the beginning of my
turning back to my Lord.

From that day on I felt a gentle pull of God
drawing me back to His Word. I read with increasing hunger. I came across Acts 1, Jesus' last
words before He ascended to heaven. The fact
that He was seen by His disciples and showed
Himself alive to them somehow became so important to me. Would He show Himself to me

again, so that I could feel His presence as I used to? Would I ever come to know His Holy Spirit and His power? Would I ever know Him as my Teacher and Comforter?

God saw my willingness and gave me true grace and courage to ask my husband to forgive my selfish ways. He forgave me and went with me to another of our children, who had been the third to try to gain freedom from home. We asked forgiveness for the way we had dominated instead of asking God's wisdom for the decisions in this precious life.

As we hugged, all of us had tears in our eyes. Gunter and I thought everything was now fine and that our child would soon come back home again. Maybe no one would even know about the whole thing or think what terrible parents we were. Satan tried right away to accuse us again, playing on our pride. Still struggling with the disappointment that "coming home" was not going to happen, we had to learn to let God have His way and will in that child's life—and in ours.

Yet while we realized God's loving hand was on us, trying to draw us closer to Him, we resented any curious questions, especially from my father. It made me irritable and defensive—almost rebellious—when he voiced suspicion and criticism about almost everything.

Then one of our children, one who had

never caused us any problem, came to us and confessed humbly and gently, "Mom and Dad, you are going to be grandparents. . . ."

Many thoughts raced through my head like a whirlwind. But then by God's grace we saw that He allowed life to come out of a first love. The reality of having a sweet little grandchild softened our thoughts.

When God's forgiving love flows through the hearts of His children, it has to keep on flowing through us toward *our* sons and daughters, who are also our brothers and sisters in Christ. Letting that old pride and reputation go, those things which seemed almost holy to me, I thought of *God's* holiness, mercy and grace, which taught me to ask, on my knees, *Lord, let me love with Your love.*

# CHAPTER 17

# *Brokenness, Forgiveness and Victory*

*And he hath put a new song in my mouth, even praise unto our God: many shall see it, and fear, and shall trust in the LORD. (Psalm 40:3)*

*A* few months after these crises our church had planned some special meetings. Nick and Betty Willems shared in our German language about the great revival movement in the West led by the Sutera Twins. Thousands of men and women were turning back to God in full surrender and repentence. Relationships among God's people were healed as forgiveness was asked and given. Peace came back to

the churches. All of this could not be hidden;
the joy in the hearts of God's children became
contagious and had to be shared with those
who were still under the burden of unconfessed sin.

*I am in too much of a mess,* I thought. *How can I
come out of this?* But I invited this couple to our
house for dinner. For the first time I felt safe to
talk to someone about our situation.

"You have to give it *all* over to the Lord," said
Betty. "Surrender your anxiety and fear for
your children. Give them over to Him."

I realized that God wanted not only to care
for one situation, one child, but *all* of them just
as they were. *What a burden would be off my
shoulders—but can He love me after I have turned
my back on Him?* I wondered.

I saw that Satan wanted to keep me from
trusting my Lord fully. As if a veil were taken
off my eyes, I saw my unfaithfulness, my independent, proud spirit and selfish desire to have
everything the way I wanted it. I broke down
before my heavenly Father, who had been so
faithful all these years, looking after us and our
children.

With the help of this dear couple, Gunter
and I started to surrender our entire situation
into God's hands, experiencing a great peace.
My anxiety settled down, and for the first time
in a long while I let God be God in my life
again. Gunter and I were willing to ask God's

Holy Spirit to search our hearts. Gently He showed us our unconfessed sin, which we had tried to correct ourselves without avail, even though I knew that only the blood of Jesus Christ could wash away my sin. I experienced the overwhelming joy of being forgiven, free from guilt and shame. Satan's accusations no longer had power over me. By faith I claimed what it says in Galatians 2:20: "I am crucified with Christ: nevertheless I live; yet not I, but Christ liveth in me: and the life which I now live in the flesh I live by the faith of the Son of God, who loved me, and gave Himself for me." It seemed too much to grasp, but I trusted in what God's Word said. His Spirit inside me would keep on guiding and teaching me. In this new relationship with my Lord, I could ask Him daily to open my understanding and show me what His will was for my life so He could make me what He wanted me to be.

In practical terms this meant dying to many ambitions in my life. I had to be willing to give up secular and even church positions. I realized that often I took credit for things God had really accomplished through me, using the gifts He had given me. I came to thank Him that I was nothing in myself, but that He was working through me and was due all of the praise. How relaxing it was not to need to reach out for recognition anymore!

God's Holy Spirit also moved through our

church, convicting us of a critical and loveless spirit. I was able to ask forgiveness for being easily offended, for trying to hide my inner hurts and pains from my brothers and sisters in Christ and not giving them the opportunity to pray for me.

One day, as I read First John 1:9, "If we confess our sins, he is faithful and just to forgive us our sins, and to cleanse us from all unrighteousness," I was deeply broken before my Father, humbled by His forgiveness, grace and mercy. There, as I confessed my sins, a joy of being forgiven flooded over my soul, overflowing in words of thanksgiving. I reached for pen and paper to write what was given to me:

> I lift my soul, Lord, up to You,
> In overflowing thanks and joy.
> How can You love me as You do,
> While I'm unworthy, yet Your child,
> My Lord, my Lord, my Savior and my
>     God?
>
> You look in mercy, Lord, on me,
> While in my trials I humbly bow.
> O Jesus, Savior, I love Thee;
> You hold my hand so sure and strong,
> My Lord, my Lord, so full of love and
>     grace.
>
> You lead my way when I obey,

And trust You always as my friend.
You're walking with me day by day,
There is nothing more on earth I want,
My Lord, my Lord, my hope, my trust,
     my all.

I could hardly believe what had happened to
me. I felt that God's grace and His Holy Spirit
was upon me. At the same time a beautiful melody and harmony filled my heart and soul. I
kept this even from my husband; I felt it was
God's ointment for my inner wounds to heal
my relationship with Him. Yet the Holy Spirit
moved me to share this experience in one of
the next meetings when I sang the song as my
testimony, very shyly, yet with joy in my heart.

Gunter and I also asked our children for forgiveness for things we had said, for our domi-
nating spirit and for playing God in their lives.
And again the next day when I was on my
knees talking to Him and confessing more sins
as the Holy Spirit convicted me, my prayer
turned again into rhymes surrounded by unknown melodies and harmonies:

When I look at my burdened heart,
I do not know, my Lord, just where to
     start.
So many things I did my way

And never asked what You would say.
And now, my Lord, I come to You;
Oh, please forgive, and yes, I know You do!
I can't believe and yet I see
That You, my Lord, in love have died for
    me.

In pride when all was looking fine,
I praised myself, that all the work was
    mine.
And self-assured, I felt so strong
But mercy told me this was wrong.

And though my heart will walk Your
    way,
I know that sometimes I may go astray,
But also know Your loving hand
Will lead me back to mercy's land.

And so, my Lord, I'm asking You,
Please stay with me, and yes, I know You
    do!
That Thy great love may shine through me,
For through Your mercy You have set me
    free.

In awe I realized that God had laid on me a new gift—to be His vessel as a songwriter. My trust in the Lord grew stronger and stronger. I felt that I could ask Him again to become more and more the Lord of my life.

We went to my father and asked his forgiveness for often being impatient, harsh and short with him. With tears running down his face, my dear father, in his late eighties, said, "The Lord also spoke to my heart. I have been quite stubborn and judgmental, not thankful enough." He also asked our children for forgiveness for being so suspicious and so critical. Under the guidance of God's Holy Spirit, a different atmosphere grew in our home.

The people in our church never forgot that Sunday morning before communion when my father slowly went to the front of the church. Leaning against the communion table, voice shaking, he asked his brothers and sisters for forgiveness. He had had a critical spirit, he said, and had not prayed enough, especially for the young people. Then an even more amazing thing happened: The young people came forward and hugged my father.

---

In that fall of 1973, I was once again in the hospital with an operation followed by serious peritonitis. The children had been at my bedside, and later that night as I was losing consciousness, I could only think, *Lord, now You have to take everything in Your hands. Whatever You want to do with my loved ones, I am ready to come home to You.* When I woke up in the early morning a voice in me said, *You are going to live.*

In the light of facing eternity, I saw all those things that had taken first place in my life as small and unimportant—my teaching at the college, the children's choir, music school. I fully trusted my Physician to bring me through. The infection suddenly started to drain out, and very slowly I started to get better. My inner peace and joy in all these experiences with my Lord flowed out of me like a fountain, and the Lord used my joyful testimony there in the hospital to witness to three people who were close to death. I prayed with two of them shortly before they left this earth.

---

Four months later our daughter Margaret became seriously ill. We found out she was born with only one kidney, which had developed a large abscess because of an obstruction in the urinary tract. We saw her barely come through the operation, and in the following years she was in the hospital more than at home. Told by the doctor that she never could have children, Margaret became very bitter against God.

"Mom, don't talk to me about God," she said. "Why does He do this to me? Why do I have to suffer all this? You don't need to pray."

Yet when she was placed twice into a bare room with a 105-degree fever, the doctors giving her little hope, I could stand there in total confidence. I left her in His care. God rewarded her own trust that developed over the years by giving her a miracle—a beautiful, healthy baby boy to join our lovely granddaughters.

———

God had yet much more in mind for our lives when in 1975, under the ministry of the Sutera Twins with the Canadian Revival Fellowship, a crusade took place in Windsor at Campbell Baptist Church, involving several churches, including our own. The Holy Spirit touched our hearts again. By God's grace He let me see the uselessness of my effort and that the only place where I would find rest was at the cross. There I must leave *everything.*

After I came home that night, the Holy Spirit continued His gentle work in me while I prayed, *Search me, O God, and know my heart: try me, and know my thoughts: And see if there be any wicked way in me, and lead me in the way everlasting* (Psalm 139:23-24).

He let me see the bitterness I still harbored deep in my heart against those who drove my parents and grandparents out of our home in Danzig-Langfuhr. I confessed this sin, and He forgave me. He allowed my bitterness to grow into forgiveness for those who had taken over our home, lived in our rooms and used our possessions—especially my grand piano.

Not long after this I saw Poland on my monthly prayer list. There people were suffering terribly. As I prayed, compassion filled my heart, and in 1989 he opened the doors for me to go to Europe. Together with my sister Edith's family, Gunter and I made it over the East German border into old Danzig, now Gdansk, in an old, borrowed van. We were never searched. Equipped with Polish Bibles, Christian literature, food, clothing and medicine, we were able to minister in two churches. Through a translator we shared what God had done in our hearts, and there was no wall between us anymore. The bond of love was real and beautiful when we sang, "Majesty, Worship His Majesty," in two languages. I knew God was pleased with His children.

———

There was hardly a day after the revival that He did not show Gunter and me things that had come between us, things we had just swept under the carpet. He worked in us to ask each other's forgiveness and make things right again. God showed me more areas where I had taken control and thought that I still had to manage things. I confessed my sin, surrendering it again to Him.

I no longer asked Him to *help* me, but to *have* me. I realized that the old self did not need any help, but needed to die. I asked Him to fill me with His Holy Spirit, and by the end of the week He became the Lord of my entire life—especially

my schedules and my overcrowded day. He became the manager of all my talents and music. I
gave Him full control so He could use me anywhere, anytime and in any way He chose. Finally a joy of total peace flooded my heart.

Gunter became my closest prayer partner;
there was no longer anything between us that
hindered our prayers. Together we brought our
loved ones before God, trusting that He would
know best how to draw each one closer to
Himself. He says in His word: "My thoughts
are not your thoughts, neither are your ways
my ways" (Isaiah 55:8); "He which hath begun
a good work in you will perform it until the
day of Jesus Christ" (Philippians 1:6).

---

One evening He showed me something
which I was hiding from Him without knowing
it. It was the fear of people, the fear resulting
from pride—I didn't want to sing the songs
that exposed my deep inner life. Until then, I
had sung alone only with my back to people,
accompanying myself on the piano or organ—
all my life I had been so afraid of singing solo I
hardly could breathe. The Lord showed me
that these songs were not only meant for *my* inner healing and blessing, but also for others.
That evening service when I shared testimony
of God's work in my life during the crusade, I
was asked to share a song. I was almost sure I

could not do it. But I realized how fear hindered my obedience. Although the grand piano was a familiar platform, I was for the first time *facing* a large audience. I called out in my heart, *Oh, Lord, help me! I want to sing for You!*

And that evening I sang a new song He had given me:

My life was crowded with many things
Important they seemed to be all,
But now the Lord has shown to me
That these things are so small.

For Jesus alone is my only guide
And His way is my best.
He leads me through darkness to see His
     light,
And there at the cross I can rest.

How often I tried to untangle my day
When Satan confused all my goal,
Until I sank down to my Savior's feet
And made Him the Lord of it all.

And though He's not lifting me out of this
     world,
His love is leading me through;
For mercy and grace are surrounding me,
And in His steps I may grow.

God continued to give me more songs while

He drew me closer to Himself. The prayers of my dear piano teacher, Fraulein Fischbeck, who had prayed over my hands, "Lord, let Magdalene's music be to Your glory only" were being answered. I was overwhelmed when my prayers of repentence turned into rhymes, not in my mother tongue but in English. Then, at the same time or a little while later, a melody with harmony filled my head with an immense force of assurance like the force behind the birth of a child. Drawn by this power to the piano, I played carefully and in obedience what was given to me. Often I broke out in tears of thanksgiving.

When Gunter came home from work, the first to hear this new creation, he would hum the bass or tenor harmony along with my playing. God had long ago planned all this for us to His glory.

Slowly I realized that these songs should be published one day, and I felt that an expert should look at them. I enrolled in the music department of William Tyndale Bible School in Michigan, where I discovered that without my knowing it, every song had a unique structure, perfectly enhancing with melody, rhythm, form and harmony the words as God had given them. Everything came from Him, was created by Him. He is the Giver of all gifts.

All my fear was gone; I now truly knew God,

in His love, had given me grace to use the gifts He had laid into my cradle.

My father was approaching his ninety-sixth birthday. While looking forward to the celebration and seeing his children come from Europe, he became very ill. Yet with all his will he tried to pull up his physical strength, which did not match his spiritual alertness. During the last weeks of his illness in the hospital, I read God's Word to him daily. His lips moved with mine—he knew passages and some entire chapters and psalms by memory. We prayed holding hands and I sang softly the hymns he loved so much. Once more I thanked him for all he had done for me and all of us, and again I asked him, "Forgive me, Papa. I am so sorry for the times when I was not nice to you and had so little patience."

His loving eyes looked at me, and he held my hand and whispered, "Love covers the multitudes of sins" (see 1 Peter 4:8).

While looking at a golden sunset shining through the open window, Gunter and I sang, "Fairest Lord Jesus." Papa stretched his arms wide as if to reach out to be freed from this earthly shell. Soon after, he entered in to see his Lord, where Mama had already gone.

During that time God drew me especially close to Himself, often waking me up at nights. I knew that I had to be obedient, so I got up to pray and read His Word. These hours became so sweet and precious that I did not want to miss them for anything.

I had been living in an intimate, loving relationship with God for a number of years, growing and learning and trusting. Yet I felt one day an unexplained sense of hopelessness bordering on depression. I prayed, *Search me, O God!* as I sometimes had done before. No sin was brought to my conscience which could have hindered my joy of close relationship with my Lord. Despite that I felt so useless, so empty. *Oh, God, what happened? What did I do?* I prayed.

Three days afterward, driving to town, I tuned to the Christian radio station and heard Charles Stanley speaking on the armor of God. I pulled to the shoulder of the road, quickly writing down His explanations of Ephesians 6:10-18. I had never paid real attention to these instructions of God's Word, but I realized that it was the evil one who tried to disturb my joy and peace, wanting to hinder my prayer and fellowship with God. Within the next two days I was led to look through a Christian magazine and a book on spiritual warfare. I knew that God was opening my eyes to understand who my real enemy was. Reinforcing my newfound fortress, I learned to put on this precious armor of God every day and knew I was in reality putting on Jesus Christ. Satan had to flee. What a compassionate God we have! He offered this protection for His children, and I had never taken advantage of this. How thankful I was to learn about Second Corinthians 10:3-5:

> For though we walk in the flesh, we do not war after the flesh: (For the weapons of our warfare are not carnal, but mighty through God to the pulling down of strongholds;) Casting down imaginations, and every high thing that exalteth itself against the knowledge of God, and bringing into captivity every thought to the obedience of Christ.

How many times since then—even daily—have I used these weapons in prayer for others and myself! "Greater is he that is in me . . ." (see 1 John 4:4).

---

Since I had surrendered our home and property, He allowed it to become a blessing to others and a shelter and peace for those who had gone through abuse and hurts in the storm of life. He tested once more my absolute trust and faith when Gunter, who was always supporting my full commitment, took early retirement after being thirty years at Chrysler and suggested that we move up north to our cottage on the lake.

I never forgot the struggle that came once more into my heart. "No way," I said. "What shall I do there—talk to the trees?" Then, walking around the backyard, I pleaded with my heavenly Father, *Lord, You have given us this place to Your glory and honor. You opened the doors for us to share and sing all around this area. Why leave it now? But I want to be submissive to my husband. Do You want another family to be happy here and also use this place for Your glory and honor? My life is Yours, as I have said before. Whatever You want to do with me, whenever and wherever You lead—I want to be in Your will—only let me not be dormant. . . . Maybe I could even minister on the nearby Indian Reservation.*

But God had much, much more in store for us. He directed and led us far beyond our wildest dreams when I stepped out in faith and let Him have His rightful place as my Master and Lord in everything.

It would burst the cover of this book to share how He freed us gradually from all the obligations which had tied us down: taking care of my father, my responsibilities in our church, many secular activities and our large property. He brought us permanently to our beautiful place in the woods, which He had so wisely and kindly provided for us the year I surrendered my entire life to Him.

We dissolved our large household of twenty years and moved into our expanded cottage up north. After I published a poem calendar and a songbook, I feared I would not have enough to do. Before I knew it, I started teaching piano again, getting involved with church and children's choirs and various Christmas programs in our little town, besides two Bible studies. Ending up in the hospital with an angina attack, I wondered, *Lord, what did I do wrong? What do You want to say to me?* The answer was clear that I had run ahead of God. Instead of resting up, I had never taken time off, a kind of sabbatical rest.

*Forgive me, Lord,* I prayed. *From now on it is just You and me again. And if You want me to be set aside only for You, as one of Your prayer intercessors, I want to be in Your will.*

After coming home from the hospital I canceled all secular activities and was fully at rest. Whatever was God's will would be for me.

We had become members of a little tourist country church, Snug Harbor Fellowship Baptist Church, which would be my place to serve on Sundays, having already received so much love and prayer support from all of them. But soon we received a call from the Sutera Twins. Could we help, they asked, in a revival crusade where God was moving among a number of churches in the Lake Erie region? The moment I heard this and repeated it to Gunter, we knew that it was God's call for us.

We live now in our beautiful place in the woods on the lake. God takes care of the landscaping, changing its dress to the most beautiful colors of the season. Most of all He watches over our home, and He opens the doors wide when He calls us to share and sing of the love that never lets His children go no matter how far they wander away from Him. He continuously teaches us to live in the spirit of daily revival: He is there for us all the time.

By letting Jesus be the Savior and Lord of your life, you too can experience this joy and peace, and you can sing with me:

> Lord of grace, I come to Thee,
> To Your cross I gladly flee,
> Praising that on Calvary
> Your blood was shed for me.
> All is done and I'm at rest,
> And my soul is truly blest;
> For I know I find with Thee
> Forgiveness full and free.
>
> Calvary, O Calvary,
> Where Christ achieved my victory!
> And now I sing in liberty,
> "O precious Calvary!"
>
> Lord, let nothing hinder me
> When I need to come to Thee,
> For my own self-righteousness

Will bring eternal death.
Nothing of my own will do
When I look, my Lord, at You;
Nothing of my own can stand
Before Your outstretched hand.

Now I'm trusting You, my Lord,
And I claim Your precious Word.
Let Your Spirit, Lord, I pray,
Guide me day by day.
O, I know I am not strong;
All my strength from You will come,
And all glory, Lord, shall be Yours
      eternally.

Calvary, O Calvary,
Where Christ achieved my victory;
And now I sing in liberty,
"O precious Calvary!"

# Recommended Reading

**Andrew Murray**
*Absolute Surrender*
   This was given to me by the Suteras and
   guided me in the right direction.
*Abide in Christ*
*The School of Obedience*
   I learned by reading through this to give
   thanks in all things, for that is the will of God
   concerning you and me as God's Word
   clearly suggests.
*Humility*
*With Christ in the School of Prayer*
*Waiting on God*
*Let Us Draw Nigh*
*Not My Will*
*The Secret of the Throne of Grace*
*The Secret of Power from on High*

**Ray Hession**
*Calvary Road*
*We Would See Jesus*
*When I Saw Him*

**Warren Wiersbe**
*Five Secrets of Living*

**R. Arthur Mathews**
*Born for Battle*

**Watchman Nee**
*Sit, Walk, Stand*
*The Release of the Spirit*